STAVE CHURCHES IN NORWAY

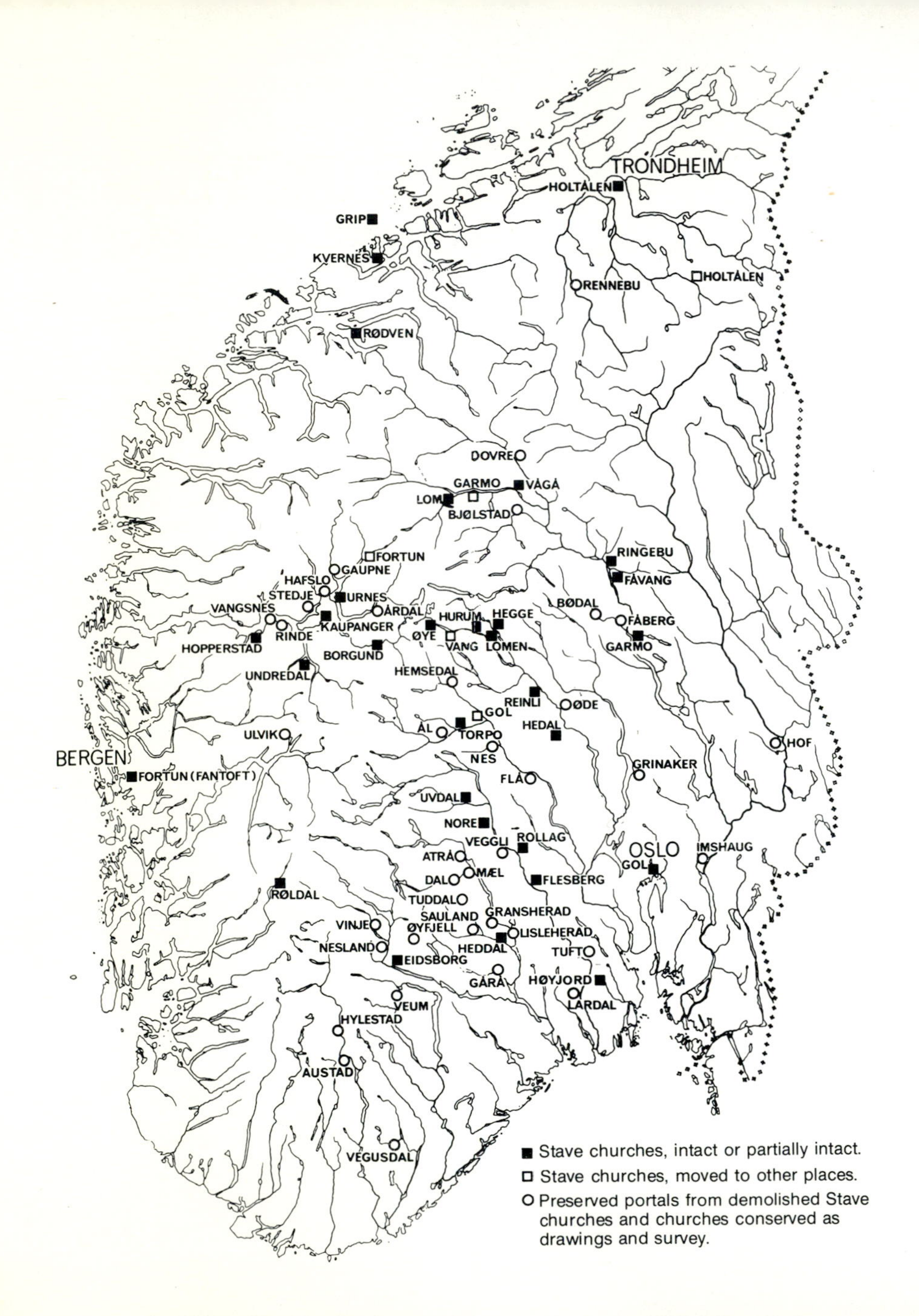

TRONDHEIM
HOLTÅLEN
GRIP
KVERNES
HOLTÅLEN
RENNEBU
RØDVEN
DOVRE
GARMO
VÅGÅ
LOM
BJØLSTAD
FORTUN
RINGEBU
GAUPNE
HAFSLO
FÅVANG
STEDJE
URNES
VANGSNES
ÅRDAL
BØDAL
HURUM
HEGGE
FÅBERG
RINDE
KAUPANGER
ØYE
VANG
LOMEN
HOPPERSTAD
BORGUND
GARMO
UNDREDAL
HEMSEDAL
REINLI
ØDE
GOL
HEDAL
ÅL
TORPO
ULVIK
HOF
NES
BERGEN
GRINAKER
FORTUN (FANTOFT)
FLÅ
UVDAL
NORE
VEGGLI
ROLLAG
OSLO
IMSHAUG
ATRÅ
MÆL
GOL
FLESBERG
DAL
RØLDAL
TUDDAL
GRANSHERAD
SAULAND
VINJE
ØYFJELL
LISLEHERAD
NESLAND
HEDDAL
TUFT
EIDSBORG
GÅRA
HØYJORD
VEUM
LARDAL
HYLESTAD
AUSTAD
VEGUSDAL
■ Stave churches, intact or partially intact.
□ Stave churches, moved to other places.
○ Preserved portals from demolished Stave churches and churches conserved as drawings and survey.

STAVE CHURCHES IN NORWAY

Introduction and survey

GUNNAR BUGGE

Dreyer

ISBN 82-09-01929-5

This publication was made possible by
contribution from Den norske Creditbank

Printed in England by William Clowes (Beccles) Ltd

PREFACE

Reliquary shrine in Hedalen stave church. The dragon heads on the gables are characteristic of Norwegian shrines. This one depicts the murder of Thomas Becket in Canterbury Cathedral.

Anyone interested in wooden architecture will be fascinated to make the acquaintance of stave churches. These, the only temples in wood to have survived in the West, have triumphantly succeeded in every respect: foreign influence has been ideally adapted to native form and to local needs, in a country with vast tracts of forest and a scattered population.

A seafaring race carried the ideas back home to their native land, and a practised hand formed them into churches. Of the about one thousand stave churches built in the Middle Age, thirty have survived, equally resistent to age and fashion.

The stave church is a sanctuary, but without the oppressive atmosphere so often found in such buildings.

Weighty tomes have been written on stave churches. This little volume has primarily a pedagogical purpose: it aims to provide a guide to stave churches for those who would like to get to know them. A *systematic* approach should make it simpler to grasp the material. Thus the reader is referred to the diagram at the back of the book, which should serve as a key to our presentation.

A comprehensive bibliography is considered unnecessary. Reference is made to the major works on this subject. It seems more appropriate to mention the names of some of those who have made a particular study of this subject, following in the footsteps of their nestor, Lorentz Dietrichson – Kr. Bjerknes and Håkon Christie, both architects, and formerly director of Ancient Monuments, Roar Hauglid, – scholars on whose work, both in words and pictures, this study is based.

The approach has throughout been intentionally matter-of-fact. The aim has been, as far as possible, to allow the stave church to introduce itself, further more to explain precisely why this very special type of architecture is to be found in Norway, of all places, and still survives.

Bærum, April 1983

Gunnar Bugge

Contents

STAVE CHURCHES IN NORWAY

Over one-hundred and fifty years have passed since the painters Johs. Flintoe and I.C. Dahl «discovered» the stave churches.

Flintoe assumed that they were «Saxon architecture», «the forerunners of the subsequently fully fledged Gothic style» (1834).

A lively discussion ensued: surely little Norway could not possibly have produced these unique buildings – or could it be the case that, in fact, this was precisely the country that had fostered such remarkable architecture?

The Roman stone basilica «recreated in wood», the centralized (Byzantine) plan church in the Near East and the pagoda in the Far East, pagan and Christian influences, national and imported styles, all these have been pressed into service to explain this architectural freak, the modest little stave church.

However, the stave church itself sets an obvious limit to the lengths to which analogies of this nature can reasonably be extended.

In stave-built architecture the timbers are placed *vertically*, differing in this respect from the log bonding technique. The problem of

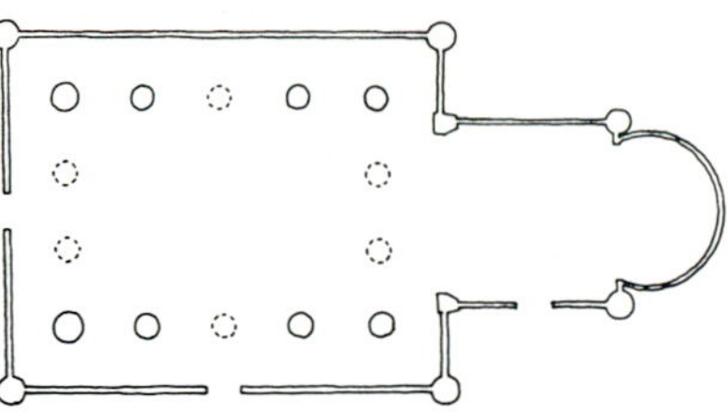

Gol stave church. Oriented on an east–west axis, as in the case of

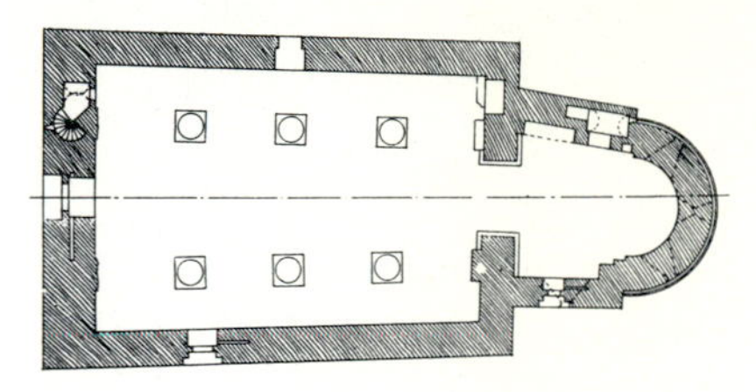

Hof, Toten, a Norwegian stone church of the basilica type.

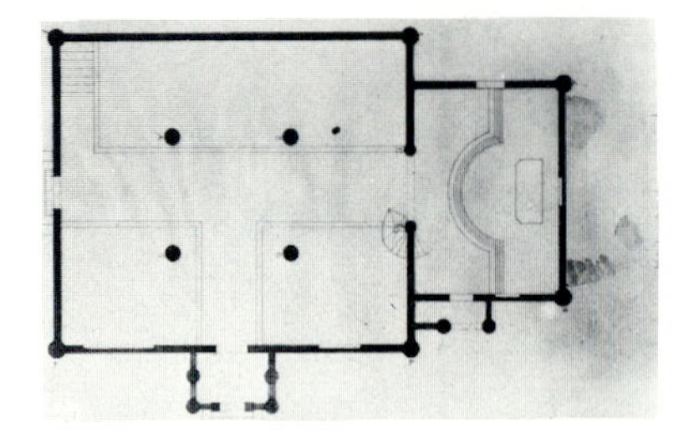

Vang stave church. The nave is almost square, as in

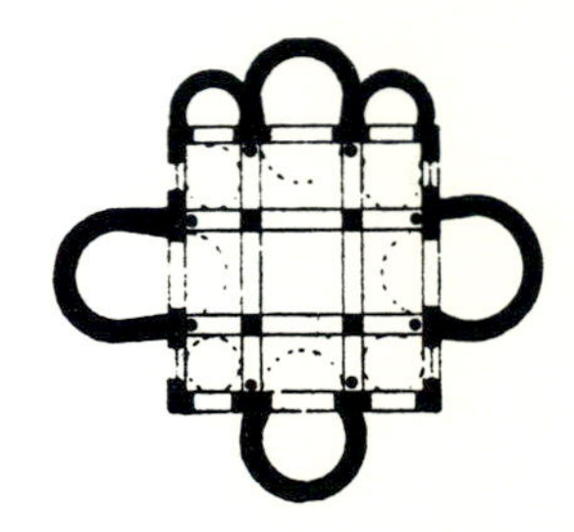

the central church at Kalundborg, Denmark.

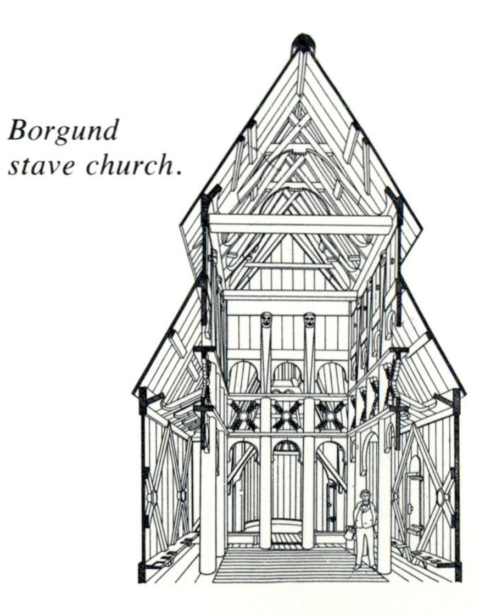

Borgund stave church.

The Daigo-Ji pagoda in Kyoto, Japan. Completed in 952. Cross-section and ground plan.

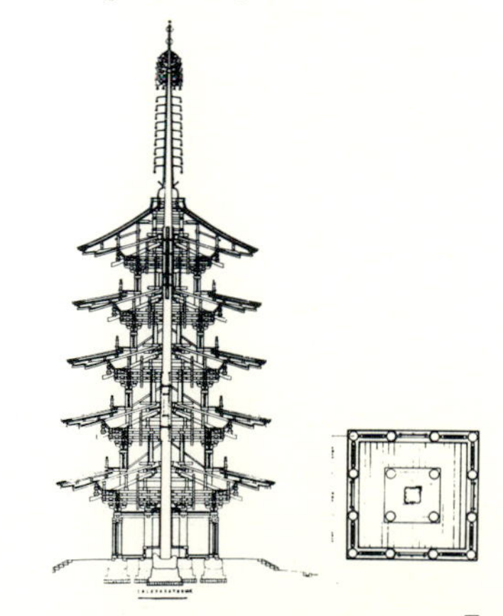

Russian log churches, Carelia. 16th century.

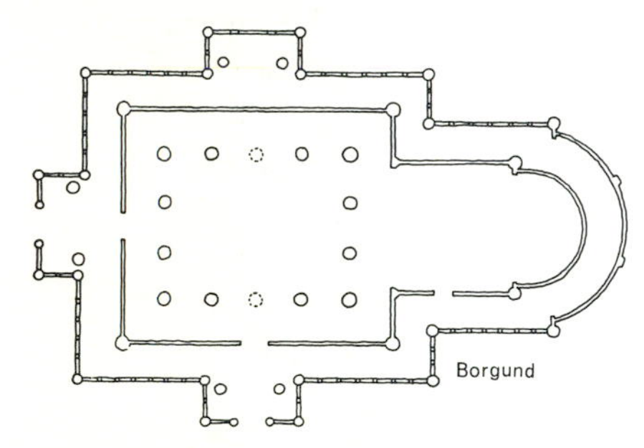

Borgund. «Open» north–south axis, «closed» east–west axis.

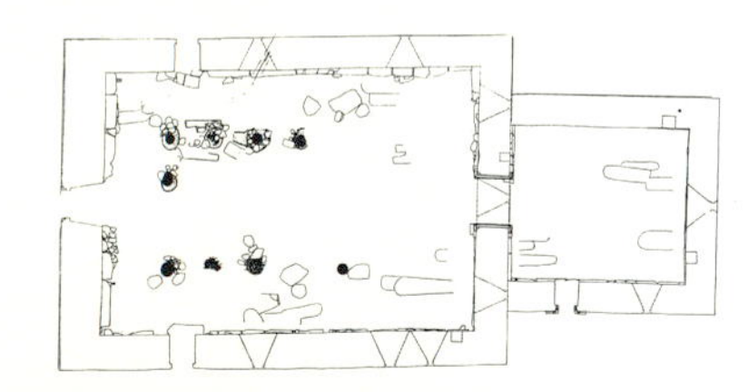

Kinsarvik, stone church with traces of earthed posts from an older stave church.

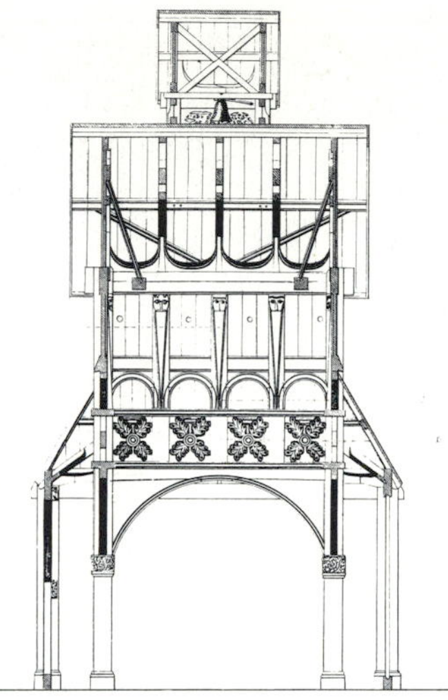

Hurum stave church showing aisles on the gable sides (east–west) as well.

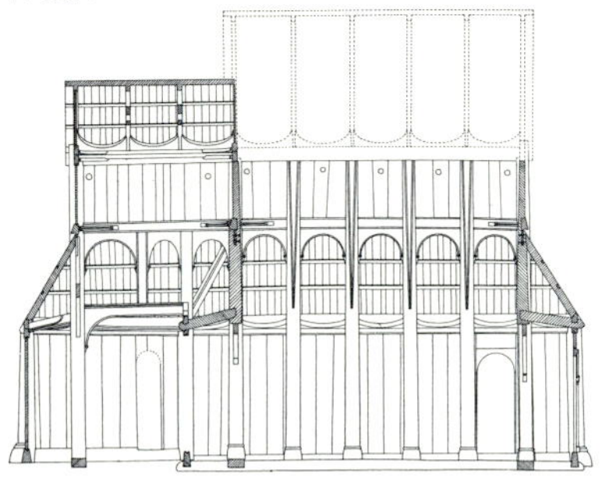

Kaupanger. Chancel addition.

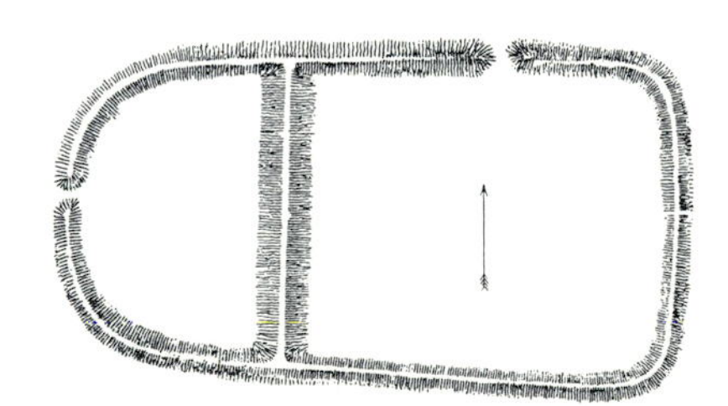

Site of pagan temple at Ljárskogum, Iceland.

stability to which this gives rise has been solved in stave churches, and particularly in the so-called «mast churches», in a very special way.

The exterior may recall the pagoda, but, with its stepped masts and ingeniously cantilevered roofs, one above the other, it aims rather at an exterior effect. In the stave church, on the other hand, the place of worship is of primary importance, with through-running free masts as much as 9 metres high.

Between the areas of the Far East, traditionally dominated by the «post and beam» construction, and the Near West lies East Europe, characterized by the notched log technique, and with ecclesiastical buildings such as the Karelian log churches of the 16th century. As Byzantine offshoots, these are churches with a centralized plan. We are reminded of the Scandinavians who colonized Russia, whenever features of the «central plan» church can be traced in the stave church – the short rectangle of the ground plan approximating to the square, the raised central room surrounded *on all four sides* by a lower ambulatory with a sloping roof. Nave and aisles in the classical sense are not involved. East-west axial emphasis is played down in many cases by doing away with masts along the sides, but retaining them on the gable ends. In fact, in the four-mast church only the addition of the chancel indicates orientation.

Undeniably, the chancel connection is the weak point in the stave church, complicating the design. It has been used to support the theory that the stave church derives from the pagan place of worship. Are stave churches, in fact, pagan temples, with the chancel added when they were dedicated to the Christian faith?

A hundred years must have elapsed between Norway's conversion to Christianity and the building of the *surviving* stave churches. So far, no definite traces of a pagan temple have been identified in this country, but on the other hand remains have been found of several earlier churches, of a primitive, earthed design.

The pagan place of worship may be assumed to have possessed important features in common with contemporary ecclesiastical building in other countries, just as the belief in the pagan gods was itself, during its final phase, coloured by the Christian faith. – The idea of the fabled Great Hall of the Saga as a precursor seems more probable. Here, too, the necessary evidence is lacking, but the ceremonial functions may have provided mutual inspiration.

Supporters of the national view have emphasised in particular the extensive use of quadrant brackets in the stave church – angle-grown, bracing members used at all levels and in all planes, as in the roof,

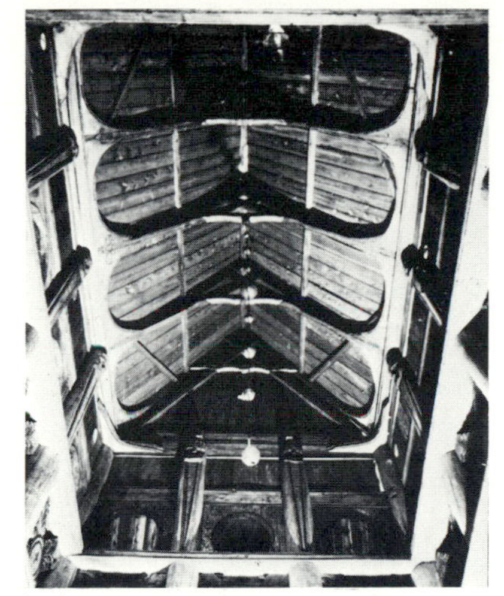

Gol stave church. Roofing with «knees» (brackets).

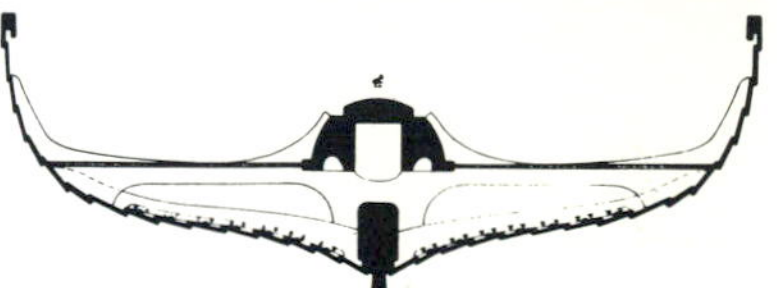

The Gokstad Viking ship.

Ensuring stability in the stave church – pressure/tension (Kaupanger). «The tough elasticity of fibre.»

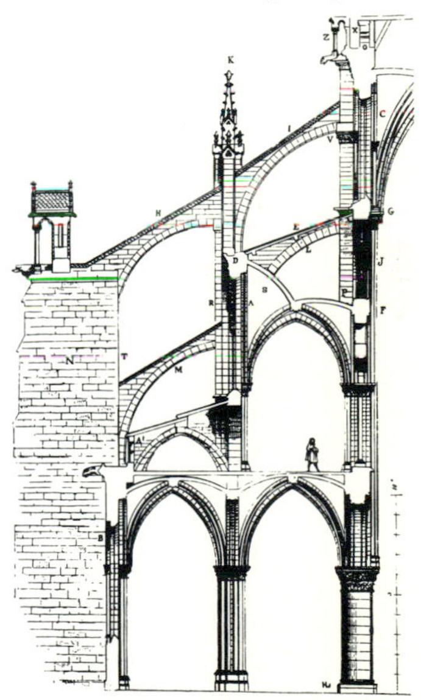

Ensuring stability in stone – weight/pressure. (Notre Dame, Paris.)

Kaupanger stave church. Masts braced against the outer walls. Above right: details of this technique.

Right: Lomen stave church. Sectional plan drawing of the bracing «collar».

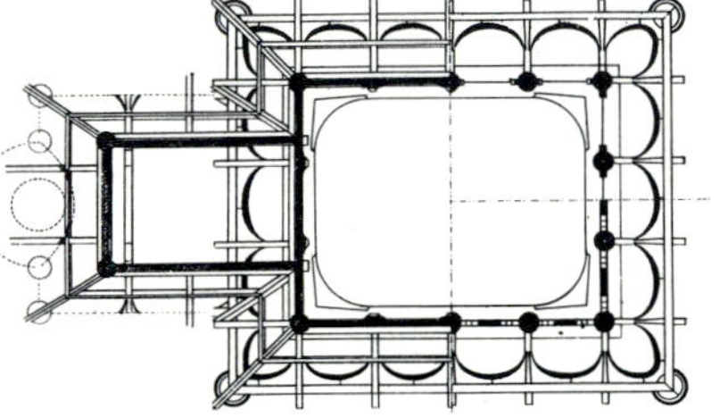

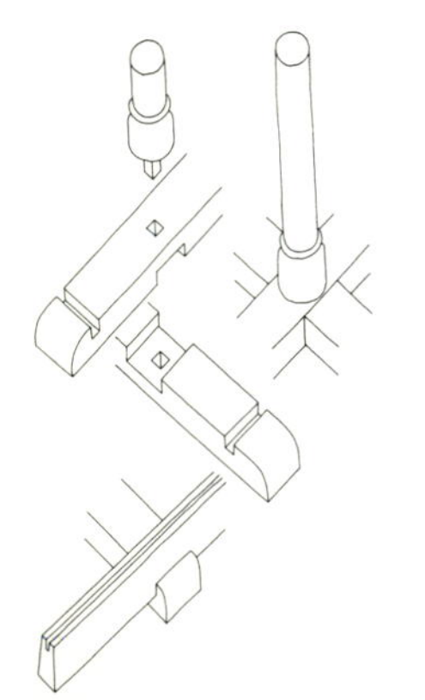

Ground frame with mast and lower bressummer mortised in grooves.

Eidsborg stave church with a pentice but no masts or ground frame.

suggesting «an inverted Viking ship».

Brackets are certainly to be found in the Viking longships, just as we find ribs in present-day boat design. But in those days there were English and Norman seafarers, too, and brackets are not unknown to us in their mediaeval houses. The roof truss with scissor braces occurs in a number of European churches in the transition to the Gothic, when a steeper pitch to the roof made this a natural solution, and the bricked vaulting demanded headroom.

However, a special feature of stave churches is the combination of brackets and scissor braces in the characteristic semi-arches between these, connecting them with the upper sill of the aisle wall. The same features recur – even in the roof of the chancel – in the small one-nave as well as in the large stave church.

In the latter the motif is repeated in the sloping roof above the ambulatory surrounding the raised central room. Both rafters and scissor braces are linked to the masts all the way round, the cut-off braces acting as aisle struts, ensuring that wind pressure is transferred from the masts to the rigid slab of the ambulatory external wall. This consists of upright 3'' – 4'' planks set in a framework of posts and sills.

This «*lace collar*» of quadrant

brackets and aisle struts (front cover) is one special feature of the mast church. Another is the *ground frame*. Both serve to ensure stability.

As a rule, stave churches without masts have no ground-frame either; instead, the outer walls are set on the stone foundation thus, imposing an extra strain on the roof bracing.

In the ground frame of the mast church the raft beams are crossed at the same level, visible in the floor, and resting on large flagstones beneath the points of intersection. At these – and frequently between them – the masts are morticed, and framed at the top. On the projecting ends (1.2 – 1.5 m) of the frame the bottom sills of the external wall slabs rest. (Axonometry Torpo). In this way the circulation of forces is ensured. The stave church is above ground, and is given stability by means of a flexible rigging system without the use of stays, a system that has survived for eight hundred years, and whose existence has never been traced outside Norway.

In Scandinavia and the northerly parts of western Europe generally «mast» churches have existed, with the masts dug into the ground. This would ensure stability, but not permanence. Masts rotted, as did too the earthed outer walls, whether these were palisade walls of thick planking, or posts driven into

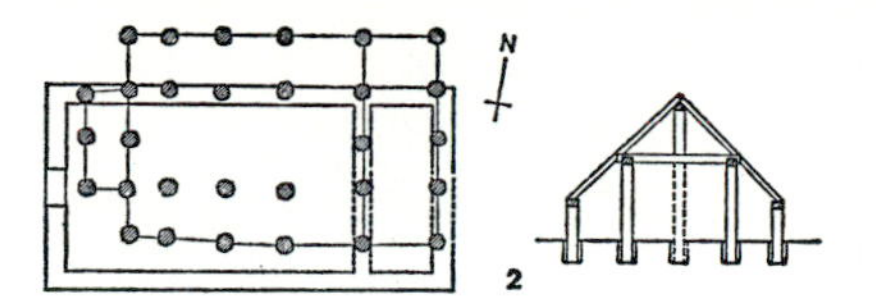

Continental wooden church with earthed posts, 7th century, St. Gallus, Brenz.

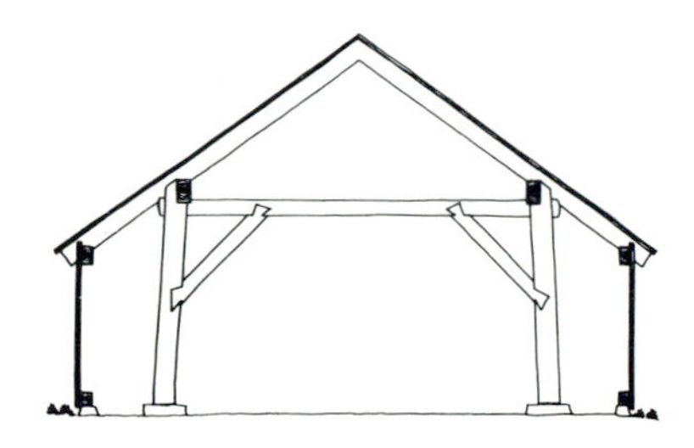

Norwegian stave-built barn, West Norway. The bearing frame is self-stabilising. The wall acts as an independent protection against the elements.

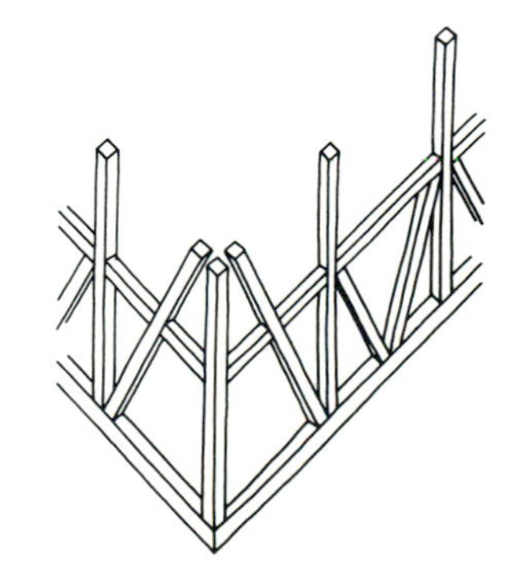

Frame technique, also with brick nogging.

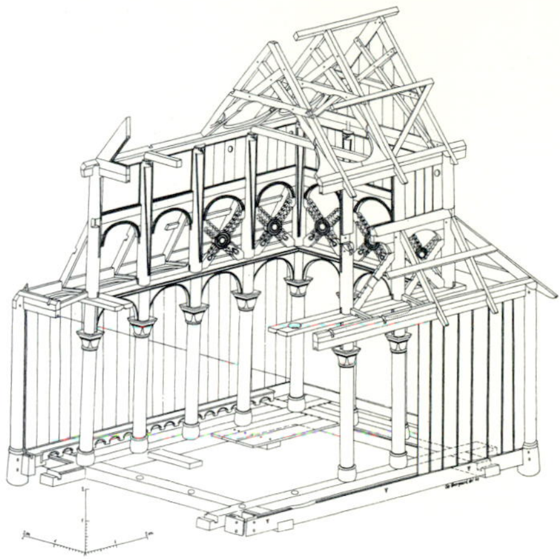

Torpo stave church. Interplay of roofing/mast system and outer walls on four sides. Wooden-building technique with features imitating stone architecture.

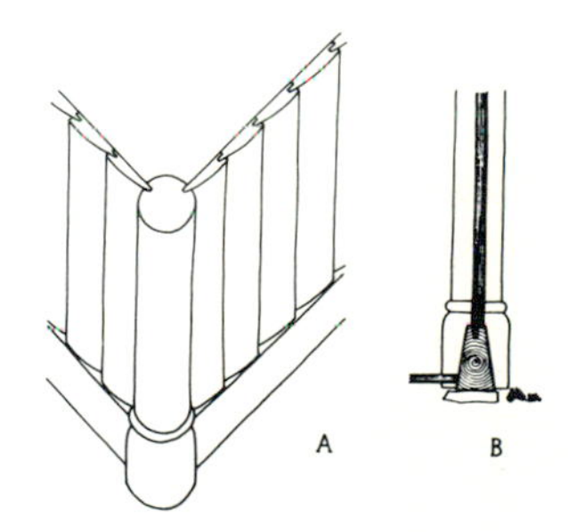

The bonded wall, of notched timbers, could be said to sag into position while upright timbers (n.p.) have a tendency to shrink. In the stave church meticulous attention to detail ensures a compact, rigid and insulating wall panel.

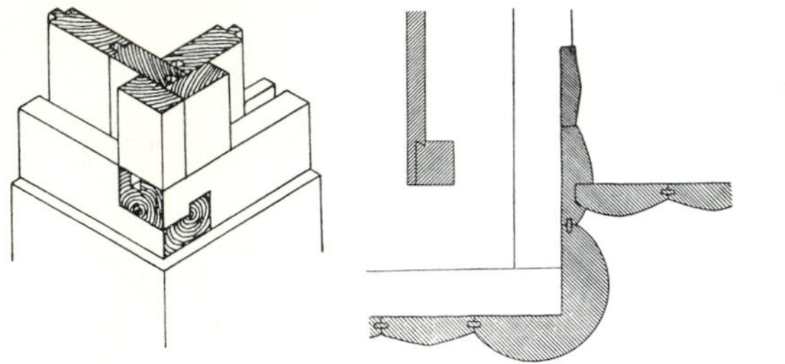

Upright timber construction (1920s). Foged Wiel, 1743: The wooden churches in Hallingdal (Flå, Nes, Gol, Torpo, Ål) are all built with «raised timbers».

Medieval stave technique, Hemse Gotland (top, middle).
W. Olsen. «Adapıed stave technique» (annex to Ringebu stave church, 1631). (Above.)

Stange. Stone, Middle Ages.

Replica in wood: Nesland stave church. Demolished 1847.

Stone replica – Hamar Cathedral.

Kaupanger stave church, colonnade in the nave.

the earth, with wall-carrying sills above ground level.

Outside Norway it looks as though at this stage the use of wood was abandoned in favour of stone, whenever churches were to be built. The stave technique then generally developed into half-timber or frame structures as employed in Norwegian stave-built barns.

In remote Norway, with its sparse population and vast tracts of forest, a land without towns, the energy that the rest of Europe expended in chiselling monuments out of stone was devoted to fashioning and developing the stave churches we so admire today.

Of a total of some two thousand churches erected in Norway in the Middle Ages, it is assumed that about one-half were stave churches. Although not suitable for ambitious projects, this in no way implies that the stave church was regarded as a second rate solution. In fact, it represented an entirely satisfactory alternative to the stone church: beeing easier to build – the technique once mastered – and large enough for the needs of our scattered rural community. Churches could be small, but there had to be *many* of them. The type has certainly proved durable, not least in the dry climate prevailing in the Fjord Country and in the valleys, where it predominated.

Based on the same technical and formal principles, the stave churches were all built during a period of some two hundred years, roughly from 1100 to 1300. Carrying out a building programme on this scale must have involved a certain amount of prefabrication, as well as specialization. A possible source of this work may have been the Inner Sogn district.

At the conclusion of the Middle Ages Norwegian wooden churches change to the notched log technique, and gradually to lighter frame buildings. Interesting exceptions are Werner Olsen's supplements in adapted stave construction from the 17th century (Lom, Ringebu, and his own building at Vågå).

It is obvious that the stave church master builders did not work in isolation – architects never do. But in drawing the line between tradition and outside influence, between «homemade» and imported, we are up against a number of missing links. Wood, after all, is less durable than stone.

On the *technical* level related finds in other parts of Europe appear almost like preliminary sketches to the Norwegian stave church, which is, after all, a late enough phenomenon to represent a crystallisation.

As a typical skeletal construction the stave church, despite some of its Norman features, can be fitted into the Gothic stylistic pattern – influenced, in turn, as the latter is by northwest European wooden architecture.

Notre Dame, Paris (Viollet-le-Duc).

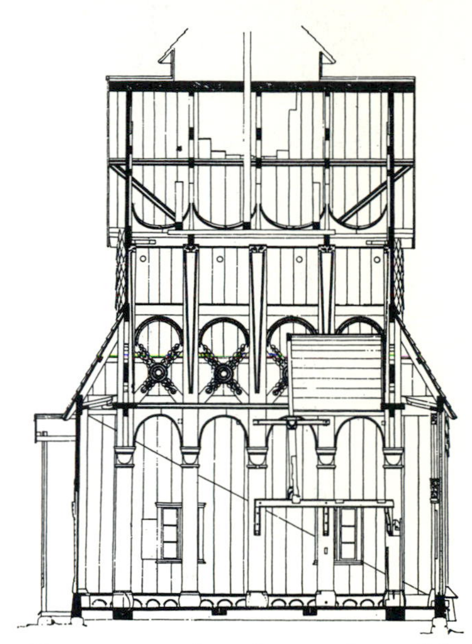

Torpo stave church, a variant of the «triforium/clerestory».

Below: Despite the similarity, the function of the pentice wall is purely protective, whereas the stave wall also helps to buttress the whole church. The pentice has «open-work» planking, for ventilation, while the stave church has a compact outer wall.

Ground sill/corner post in a stave church.

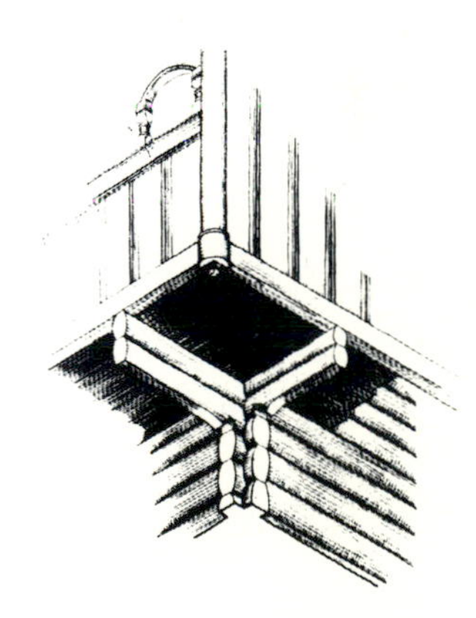

Notched log corner/pentice of a loft.

Hedalen – west door.
Below: Sketch for positioning of door.

It may be assumed that in the 12th and 13th centuries the tradition of building in wood was strong, and independant, in Norway. During this period the interaction between stave and notched log techniques, which was to distinguish all our wooden architecture right down to the 19th century, arose.

We are faced during this period with a technical skill which allowed experiment and new ideas; at the same time we had a wealth of models, distant enough to ensure stylistic freedom and scope for imagination.

We are still compelled to establish a literary basis for the royal Great Hall, the pagan «hov» (temple), and an archaeological basis for the Pan-European stave church, beneath the ground.

As long as these remain «buildings of the imagination», and formal dependence of the stave churches on outside influence is as debatable as it is, we must in this book consider them *original works* – the Norwegian answer to the challenge of mediaeval church.

The *portals* comprise an integral part of the outer wall of the main room. Like the wall planking, the lateral planks of the portals are slotted into upper and lower sills, while the top piece is in turn braced between the lateral boards.

As a rule, there are entrances of equal size and importance to the west and the south of the nave and frequently, too, a smaller one leading to the chancel.

With their wealth of ornamentation the portals stand out from the otherwise unbroken wall surface.

Like the stave church itself, the portals reflect the tension between the native and alien. The opening itself is flanked by easily recognisable features of classical architecture: semi-columns with base, capital, and archivolt. The intricate and curious animal and plant carving on the barge boards, originating at the base and culminating in the contending dragons above the archivolt, provide a dramatic foil to the rigid main theme.

Apart from those to be found in surviving stave churches, a number of portals have been preserved in museums.

System of dragons (Flå).

At the back of the book will be found a diagram which aims to explain schematically the origins and mutual relationships of the stave churches.

The two *vertical* columns show the two main types: on the left the small single-nave *A-type* without masts, and on the right the large *B-type* with masts for supporting the walls in the raised central portion.

These types have a common origin in northwest Europe's traditions of wooden architecture, but may also be said to have their parallel in churches in stone (single-nave, respectively basilica).

Like their counterparts in stone, the stave churches have a rectangular chancel, somewhat narrower than the nave, but as a rule their chancels and naves have walls of the same height. The apse (a semi-circular annexe to the chancel) is a common feature in the south-eastern parts of Norway.

In the wooden church additional attributes include the pentice and belfry, both loose and subsequent adjuncts without any constructive significance. A few have also in time acquired a free-standing steeple, or stave-built belltower above the west entrance.

Of the *A type stave churches* a corresponding number, apart from their corner posts, also have intermediate posts in the walls. A few have a central mast, whose purpose

«A» TYPE

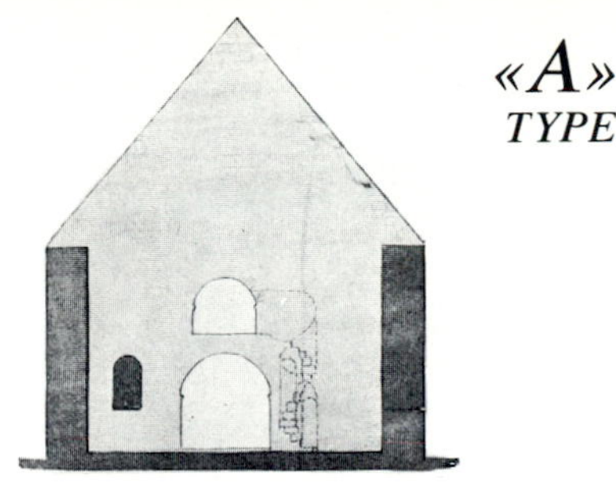

Rygge, stone, single nave.

«B» TYPE

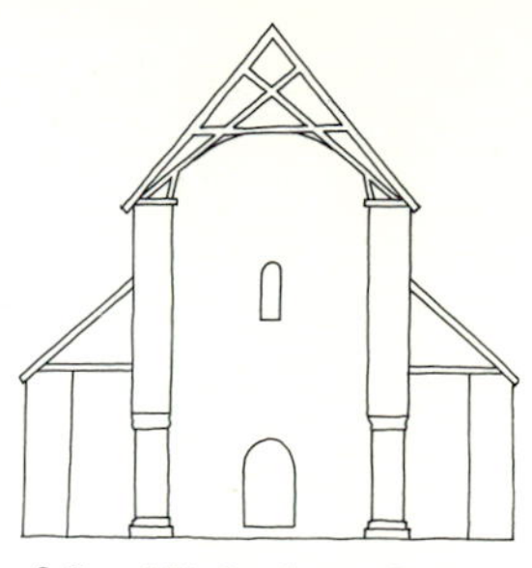

The church of St. Nicholas, Gran. Below: Urnes stave church, corresponding sectional drawing.

Botne, stone.
Vangsnes stave church.

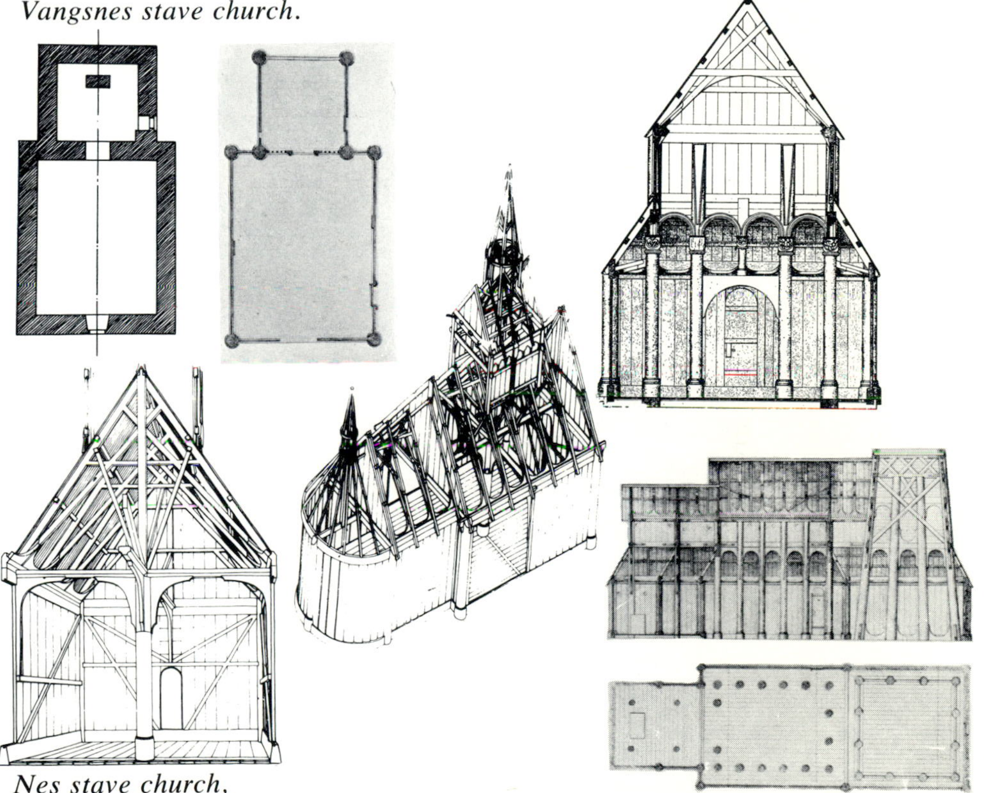

Nes stave church, with central mast (reconstruction).

Årdal mast church, with tower at the west end.

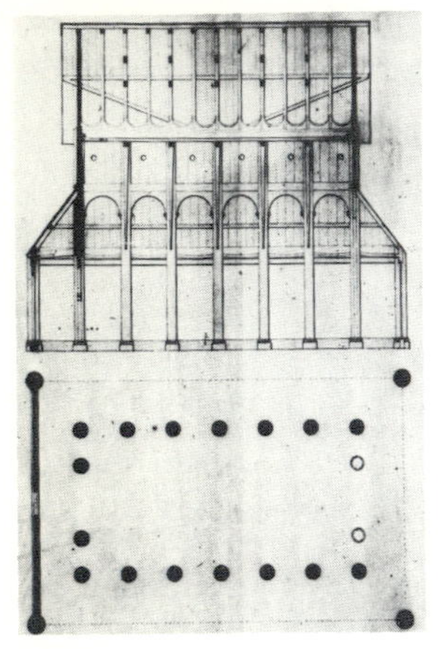

Hafslo stave church (demolished) a representative of the Kaupanger group.

Hopperstad: Nave wall, stone-imitating details, cross braces.

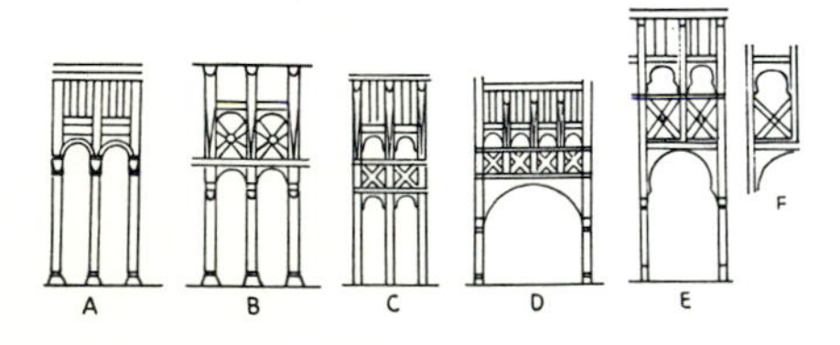

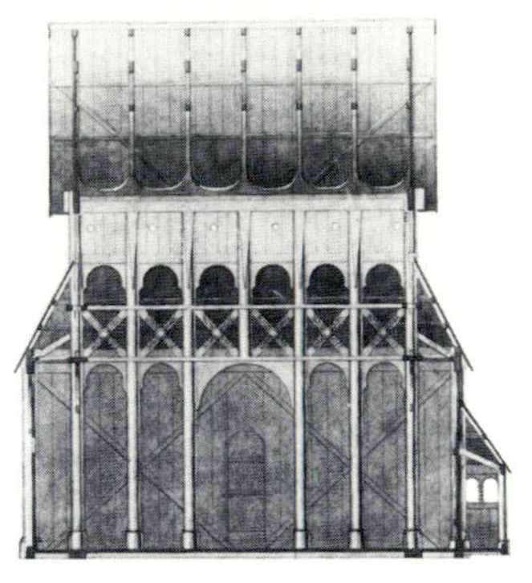

Stedje stave church (demolished), a representative of the Borgund group.

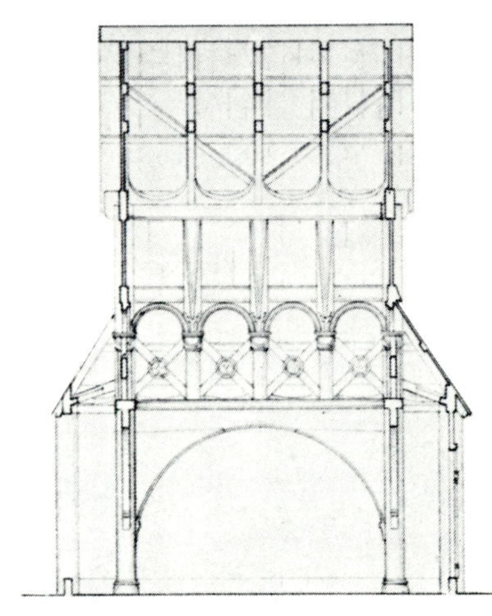

Grinaker stave church (demolished). The intermediate masts may have been cut at a later date (cp. Hurum/Lomen)

Sections of longitudinal walls in A. Urnes/Hopperstad/Lom/Fortun/Kaupanger, B. Torpo, C. Borgund/Gol, Hegge, D. Hurum/Lomen, E. Ringebu, F. Heddal.

is to support a belfry that is often of considerable height. For this reason the central mast must be braced against the bressumer of the outer walls, based on a principle somewhat different from the masts in the B-type churches.

Among the *mast churches* a distinction may be made between the Kaupanger group and the Borgund group.

Churches in the *Kaupanger group* have a complete row of masts, in fact a colonnade, running lengthwise.

Details in imitation of stone architecture, such as capitals and a marked archivolt, add to the illusion of a basilica. In this group Hopperstad and Lom both had subsequently added bracing members inserted, of a kind otherwise characteristic of the *Borgund group*. These consist of cross-braces, inset between string beams, i.e. double beams nailed together and keeping the masts in position, just over halfway up.

Using this system the cutting of masts was optional; these could rest on the lower beam and be held in place by the upper one. At the same time a certain triforium-effect was achieved. This idea is developed to its extreme in the four-masted Valdres church, where the row of masts, 14 in all, is complete in the upper part of the nave. (Front cover).

In the interiors of the Borgund

group the traditional ecclesiastical motifs are less in evidence; here, wood speaks its own unmistakable language, undeniably more pagan in tone, with the masks at the top.

A church such as *Torpo* must be assigned to a type midway between the two groups.

In other respects the mast churches are structurally all of a piece. The church at *Øye* may, however, be regarded as representing a type of its own, a link between types A and B.

The three *horizontal* columns indicate the principal technical stages chronologically: the upper one represents the primitive pan-European earthed stage, the middle one the same with the added improvement of a ground sill placed above ground-level, the lower one the final stage, where the entire structure is raised above the earth, and rests on a stone foundation.

In Norway we have no examples as yet of the A or B type in stage 1, as exemplified by Greensted in Essex and St. Drotten in Lund. Both have earthed palisade walls, the latter with earthed free-standing masts.

Excavations beneath the floor of the stone churches now standing in Mære and Kinsarvik, the vanished Church of St. Mary in Oslo, and under the stave church now standing in Kaupanger, have brought to light remains of wood-churches with earthed posts, whereas the

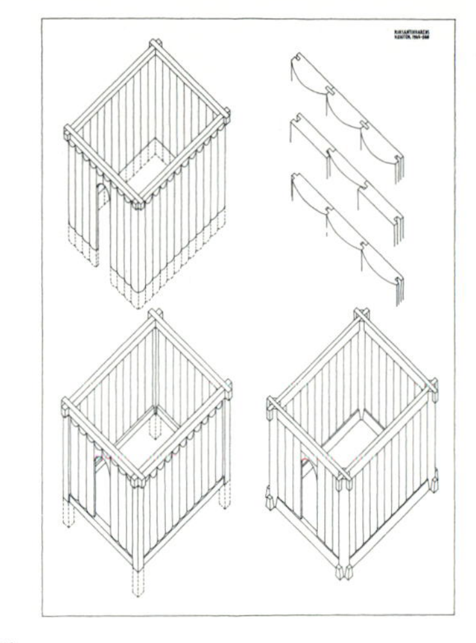

Three stages in stave construction: earthed wall, earthed posts, the entire structure above ground.

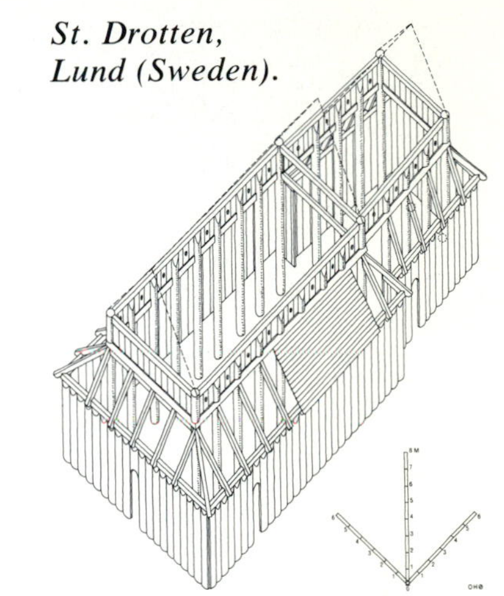

St. Drotten, Lund (Sweden).

Earthed mast church.

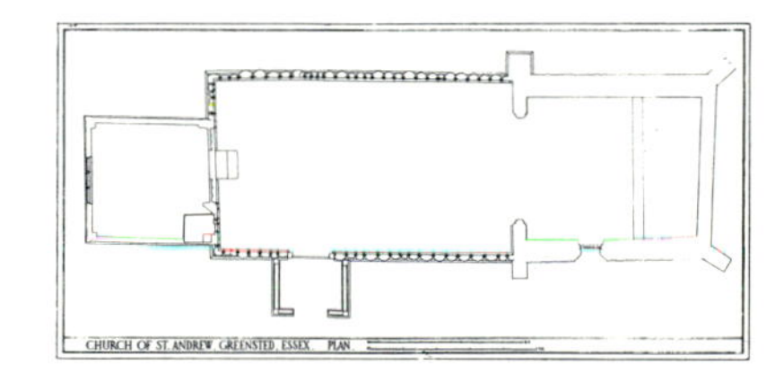

Greensted: stave built section left.

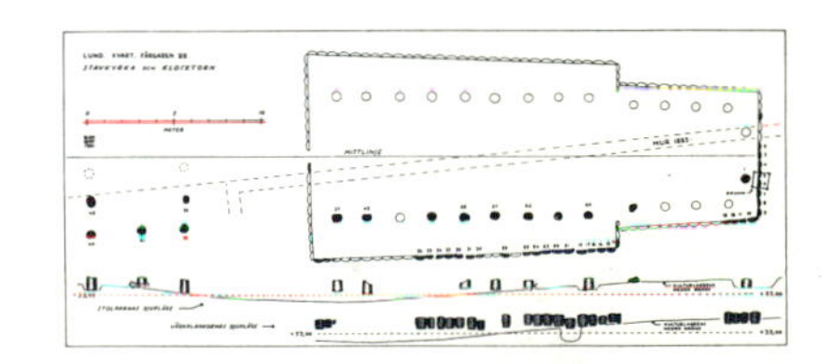

Plan of St. Drotten.

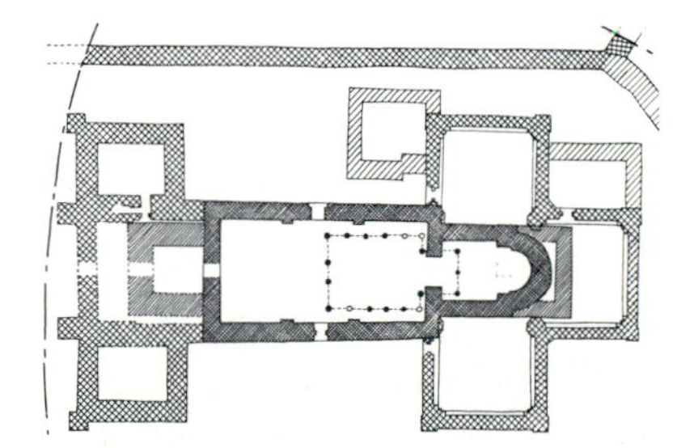

The Church of St. Mary in Oslo, showing the stave church and the two subsequent stone churches.

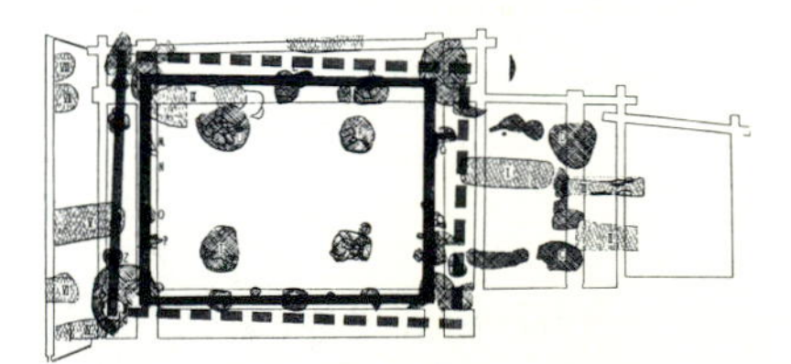

Urnes: post holes beneath the present stave church (H. Christie, Knud J. Krogh).

Hemse Church, Gotland. Reconstruction.

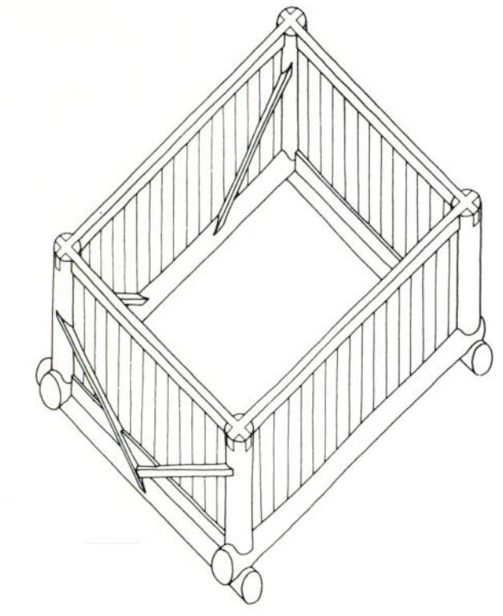

Stave building from excavations on the Bergen quays. Clearly separate frame and «filling» (H. Christie).

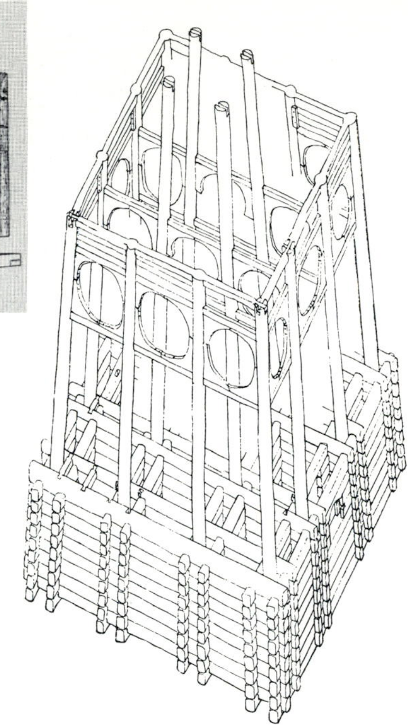

Häverö, Uppland. Steeple from the 1600s showing «unconventional» mast construction.

walls are assumed to have rested on sills above ground-level, inset between the posts (Column 2A).

Traces of earthed posts beneath the present Urnes church indicate that there were four free masts in the nave, and posts in the longitudinal walls, all earthed. Here the sill beams, too, seem to have been inset between the posts, above ground level. Similar finds have recently been made under the stave church in Lom (q.v.). Both finds have tentatively been listed in Column 2B.

To the third stage belong all the surviving stave churches in Norway, these being our chief concern in this book.

The «special Norwegian features» listed apply, or have applied, to all of them.

These characteristics cannot be applied to related Swedish «bressummer» churches, which are listed under 3A, or to an extant alternative interpretation of Urnes I.

In many cases the «Gothic attributes» are not original, and for this reason are placed at the bottom of the diagram.

Bottom: Borgund stave church (left) in its original (romanesque) guise. Pentice and ridge turret as at Eidsborg (right) are «Gothic» additions.

Edvard Munch: Cathedral in the forest.

Systematic Description of the Stave Churches

Scale: see comparative plans p. 82–84.

1. HOLTÅLEN

This church was moved in 1884 from Gauldalen to Sverresborg, near Trondheim. It is first mentioned in 1345.

In all its simplicity it may be taken as a prototype for the «single-nave» church. The rectangle formed by the nave measures just over 5 x 6 m, that of the chancel being proportionately smaller, approximately 3 x 3½ m, but with walls of the same height as in the nave. The frame of the outer wall consists of a trapeze-shaped sill beam, placed on edge, round cornerposts which, with their powerful bases – in this case spherical – overlap the notched sill beams, and the bressummer. The latter is in two parts, the lower member, like the sill beam, having a groove into which the wall planks are fitted. The upper member, with its complicated oblique profile, serves both for bracing the wall, and supporting the roof.

This has scissor braces, interlinked and connected with the upper bressummer by means of quadrant brackets. In this way the roofing contributes actively to stabilizing the structure.

In most stave churches of the A type we shall discover, covered by subsequent camouflaging alterations, a mediaeval core similar to the one we can study at Holtålen.

A variant often encountered is provided by one or more intermediate posts in the longitudinal walls.

The rafter principle at Holtålen is also to be found, with minor deviations, in the roofing above the raised central room in the mast churches of the B type.

The scissor rafters, with their ingenious quadrant bracket links, may have provided the inspiration for the solution involving buttressing transverse struts beneath the sloping *roofs* of the ambulatory in mast churches. (See introduction, p. 9–10).

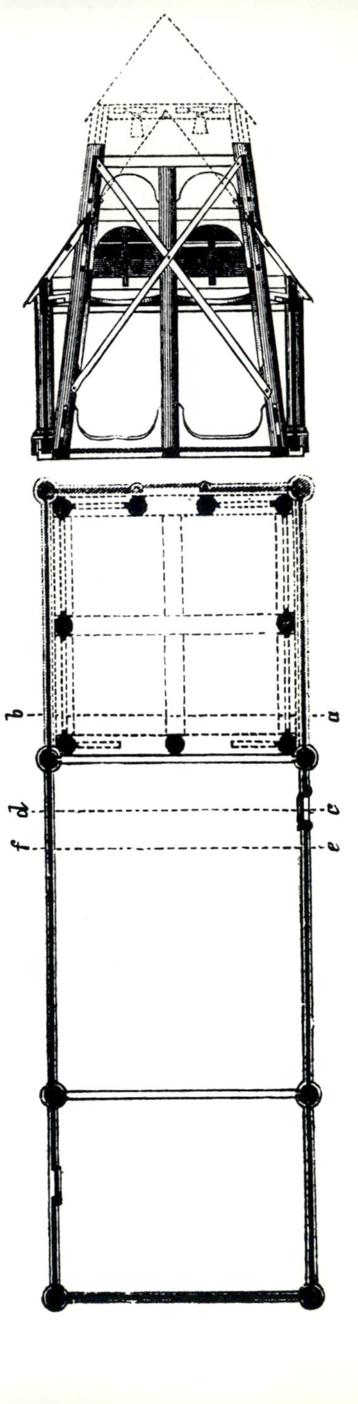

Right: Rinde stave church (demolished) with a tower above the west door. See introduction: Årdal.

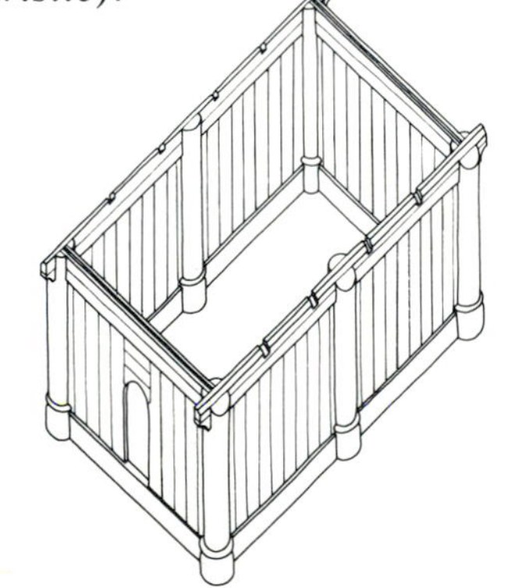

Below: Stave church with intermediate posts set in the walls (H. Christie).

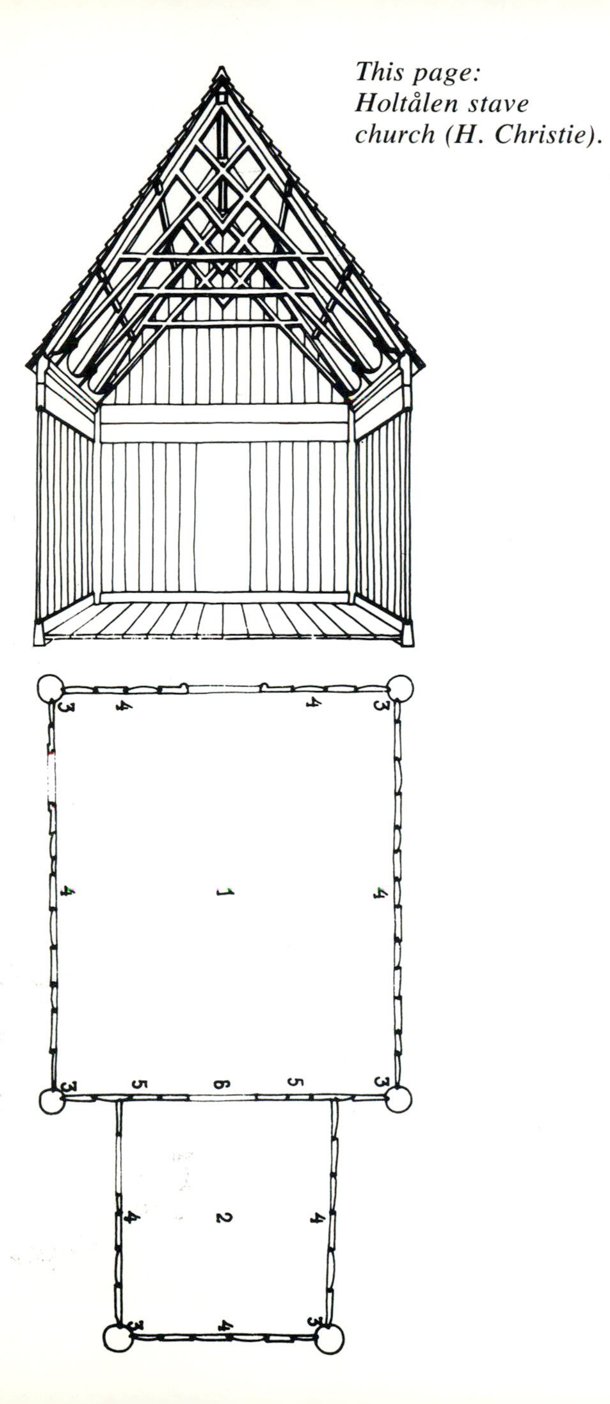

This page:
Holtålen stave
church (H. Christie).

2. UNDREDAL

In this remote spot, still accessible only by boat, this panelled stave church, painted white, is to be found in the very heart of the community. The stave-built forward portion of the nave measures some 3.8 x 5.3 m. This is Norway's smallest stave church.

The round posts, the sills and plank walls of the mediaeval portion are clearly seen in the interior. The original roof structure has been preserved over the barrel-vault ceiling, which may have been added in the 1700s.

This church was investigated for the first time in 1902 by the architect Jens Z. Kielland. The plan drawing shown (after Gerhard Fischer) indicates the medieval portion by hachuring. The walls decorated in the Renaissance were painted over, but have now been uncovered.

The present chancel is log-built, and although somewhat lower has the same width as the nave. At the west end a steeple has been added, supported by square-cut masts, standing free inside the outer wall, which runs flush with that of the the nave, and is built in a somewhat more primitive stave construction. The porch is built with vertical timbers.

There are signs in the wall that the church at one time had a gallery in the nave, and later as well in the annexe to the west, right down to the 1860s.

The date 1447 (of doubtful origin), carved above the mediaeval profile in one of the rafters, may indicate a subsequent repair to the roof, and possibly too the year when the steeple was added.

No traces are to found of an alleged pentice (mentioned in 1665).

Items of inventory to be mentioned are the pulpit from the middle of the 17th century, and the unusual candelabrum adorned with carved stags' heads.

The original dark sanctuary now has two ogive windows in each longitudinal wall, and one in each chancel wall.

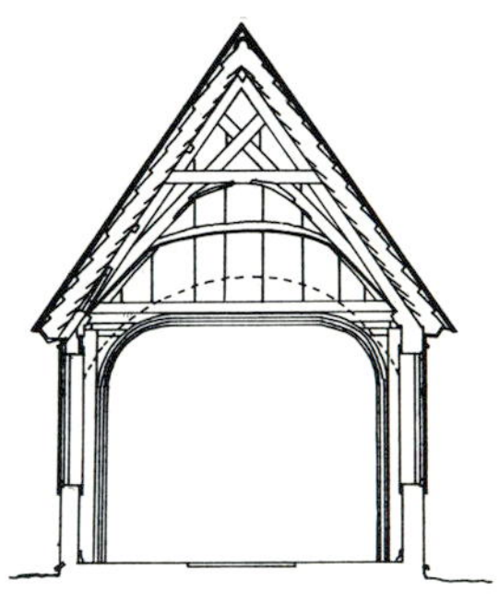

Right: looking west, showing the square-hewn, detached posts supporting the bell tower.

3. ROLLAG

This church originally had a stave-built chancel with an apse, probably a pentice running round the entire building, and possibly a central mast, like others in this valley.

Today, all that remains of the mediaeval structure is the four round cornerposts in the nave, and fragments of the stave construction in the longitudinal walls.

In 1666 a new, wider chancel of notched timber was erected, and windows were inserted. During the years 1697–99 the central portion of the longitudinal walls was pierced, and wings added in raised timbers. This conversion was beautifully executed, in the same way as in the large churches of Gudbrandsdal, in the spirit of stave building: square-hewn posts and sills, with planking inbetween, some of which derives from the earlier stave walls. The galleries in the transepts were added in 1702. The vestry was erected in 1739.

During the incumbency of Parelius (1752-73) the entire church was raised with the addition of four rounds of logs, and the nave extended to the west. These alterations illustrate in a interesting and convincing manner the possibilities of combining the stave and log techniques. At the same time the church acquired a ceiling composed of joists, as well as a porch, and a belfry on the roof.

Parelius had ceiling and walls painted over with the blue colour that still predominates inside. The restoration of the church in 1933 revealed the 17th-century decorations in the chancel, which may have been inspired by the wall decor in the demolished chancel, similar to those in Nore and Uvdal stave churches.

The baroque altar panel was donated to the church by the then vicar, Winther, in 1670. The church also contains a crucifix of a late-Gothic type, as well as a rococo pupit painted in 1763.

Beneath the chancel was a timbered burial chamber. Inside was discovered the large stone cross now standing outside the church. The wooden gateway dates from1723.

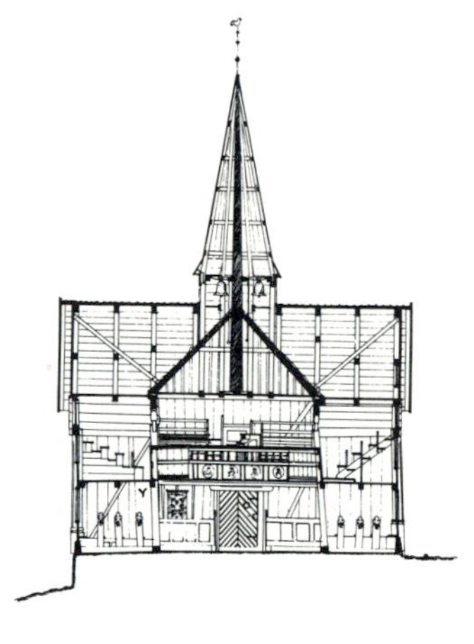

Sectional drawing and exterior clearly show the bonded logs on top of the stave-built walls.

Below: wooden font with lid.

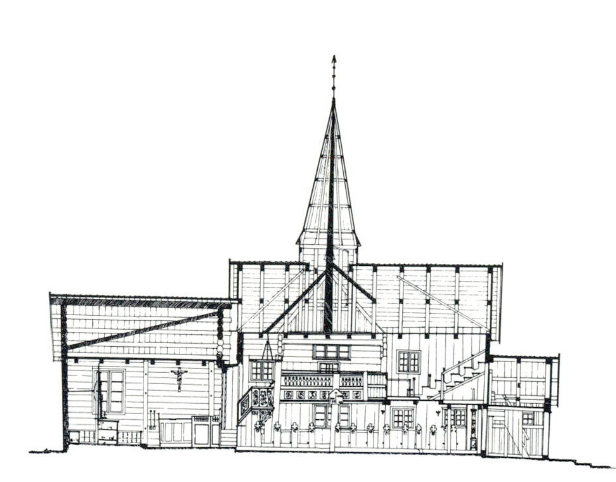

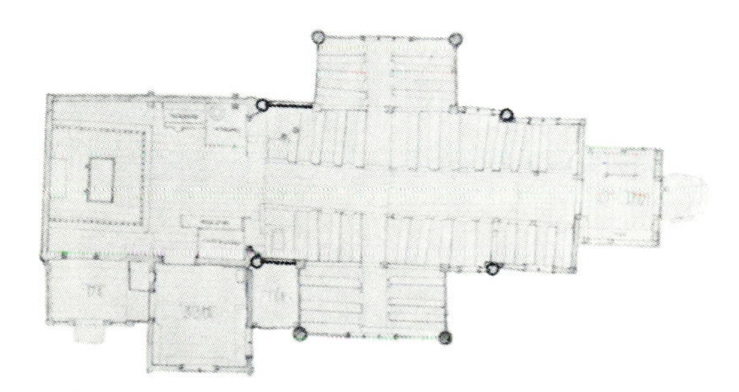

4. REINLI

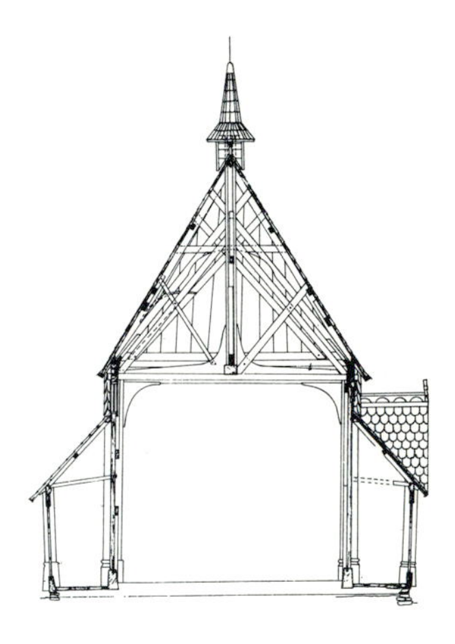

Above: the powerful buttressing of the «King post» (or «suspended» central mast) can cope with more than the present belfry.

We have seen that in more recent times a number of stave churches have had their chancel extended, as a rule to the same width as the nave. In Reinli, a later church probably from the Gothic period, nave, chancel, and even apse have been given the same width, if not originally, at any rate shortly after building. Differences in the edge moulding of planks in nave and chancel would suggest that there were two building stages.

This unusual stave church has its distinguished parallels in the large single-nave hall churches of the Gothic period on the Continent, such as the Sainte Chapelle in Paris.

Between the nave and the chancel was an openwork rood screen, now no longer there, but shown here in the cross-sectional drawing of Georg Bull' reconstruction.

Round the entire church runs a pentice, supported on the projecting ends of the building's ground frame and not – as elsewhere – a structurally independent addition. Consequently, like the wide chancel and apse, the ambulatory, too, was probably part of the original building, although this does not quite tally with the fact that the walls of the nave are weathered, and must therefore have remained for some time without the protection of a pentice.

The exposed mediaeval floor reveals the ground frame as a network of intersecting beams, on the same lines as in the large mast churches. Strangely enough, the lower sills are morticed into the cornerposts, which are firmly set on the foundations. This system is known to us from simple stave churches of the A type.

Reinli has no free masts, but in the open roofing we find a «suspended» central mast, resting on one of the five transverse beams, and braced by brackets and struts in all four directions. Though technically sophisticated and highly effective from a spatial point of view, the present roof turret by comparison, cuts a rather sorry figure. The original height is not known, but a new mast-tree 15 metres long was erected in 1685. When this was subsequently destroyed by lightning, the belfry was placed straight onto the roof ridge.

Details is imitation Gothic are a feature of the three entrances and of the pentice.

Pulpit, altarpiece and an organ gallery in the apse from 18th century. About 100 years ago a west gallery was installed, as well as a new floor with benches, and windows with small panes. At a recent restauration these windows remained, the gallery and the new floor with benches were removed.

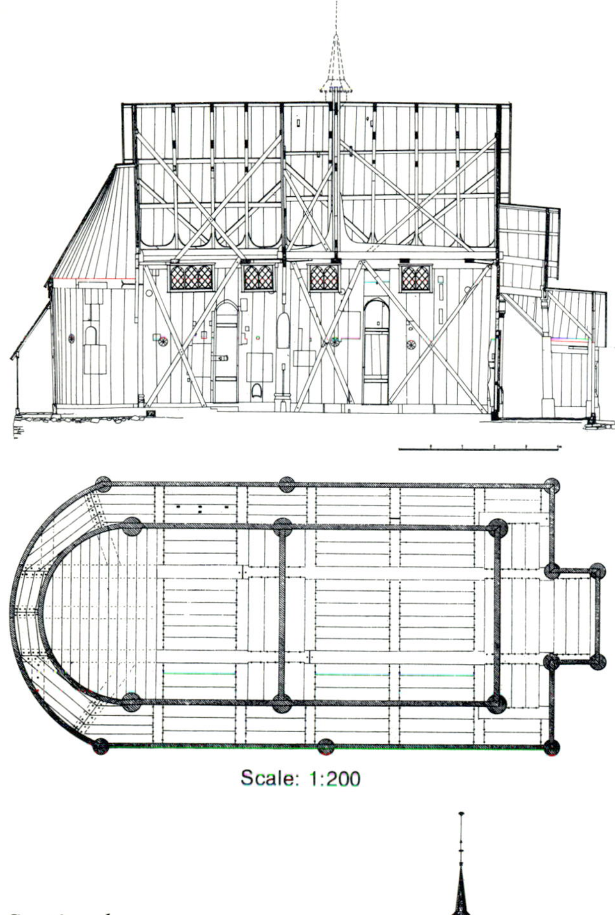

Section by Georg Bull, showing rood screen.

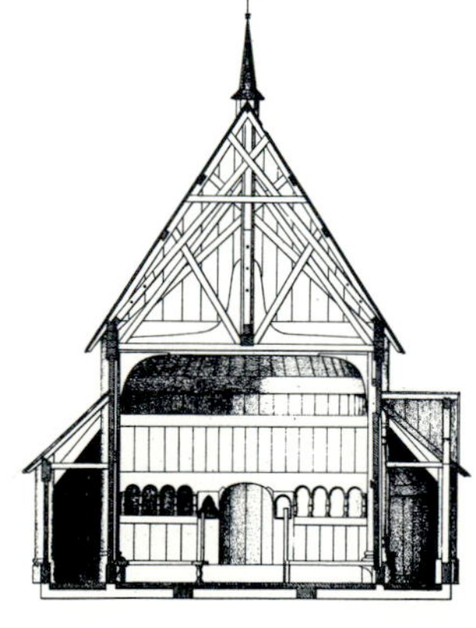

5. HEDAL

The nave, surrounded on three sides by a pentice, is from the Middle Ages. Before its enlargement and conversion to a cruciform church in 1699 Hedal had a narrower chancel with an apse, in common with so many related churches of the A type.

The magnificent west doorway, which does not show to advantage in the darkness of the pentice, displays close kinship with Hopperstad and Borgund, and enables us to place Hedal as early among the Valdres churches.

However, this church has borrowed an advanced structural feature from the mast churches, viz. the ground frame. The sill beam in the outer wall rides over the cantilevered ends of the ground frame (see plan). This gives the skeleton far greater stability than the ordinary system used in the A type, where no frame carries the sill beam, which rests directly on the stone foundation.

In other words, there is one structural line to be traced running from the multi-mast via the eight- and four-mast churches (Gol/Hegge – Hurum/Lomen) and Reinli, with its «suspended» central mast, to Hedal, where finally masts are entirely omitted.

In the considerably later church at Reinli the pentice sill beam likewise rests on the projections of the foundation frame. In Hedal the pentice is structurally independent, as in other cases usual. It rests on the stone foundation, leaning against the walls of the nave in order to protect them, just as it protects the congregation against the rain. In this church, as at Reinli, keyhole-shaped squints in the pentice are a striking feature.

The roof truss, with its scissor braces and bracket bracing, is part of the original building.

Apart from the doorway, the church is renowned for its reliquary, depicting the martyrdom of Thomas Becket, and for its triptych, with a crucifix and subsequent rose-painting. A 13th-century madonna, which has been preserved, was at one time kept in the triptych.

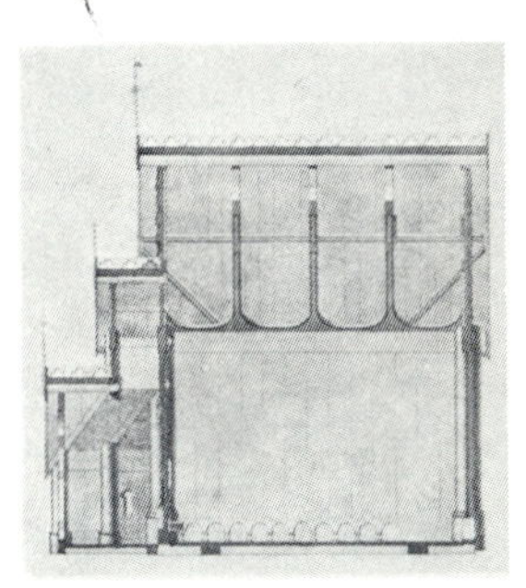

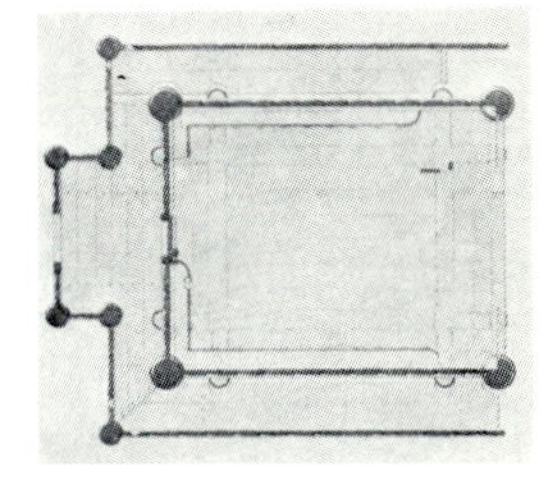

Wash drawings show the remaining medieval portions. Reliquary: see preface. Portal: see p. 14.

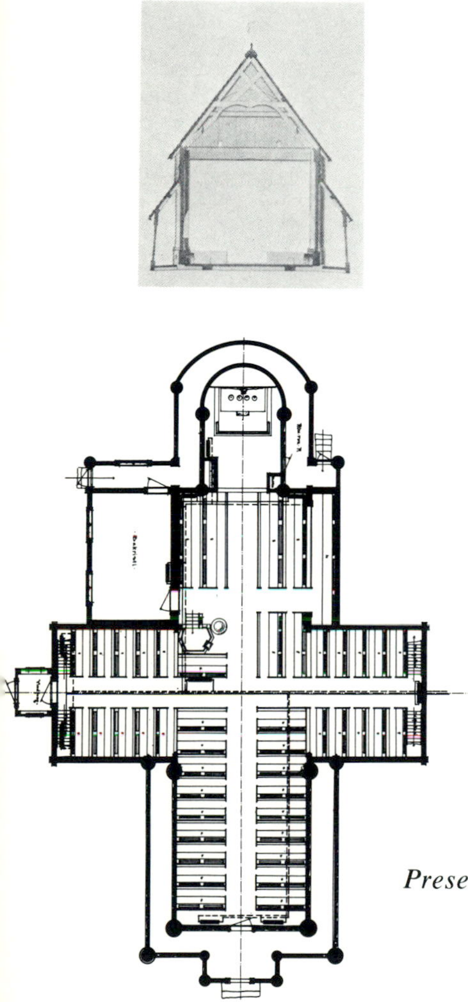

Present plan.

6. EIDSBORG

This church is very similar to that at Hedal: as in the latter, the nave, with its pentice, of about the same size and shape, has been preserved from the Middle Ages. One essential difference is that Eidsborg has no ground frame, as is usual when we are dealing with the A type. The pentice, which is structurally independent, may be contemporary with the church itself.

The extensions at the east end (log-built extension of the nave in 1826, the present chancel 1845) are, however, of a less imposing size in Eidsborg; also, with the ridge turret in position, we have more of the original proportions and appearance. One striking feature is that the roof, posts and walls are clad with shingles. In the west gable, in fact, use is made of a shingle-imitating panel.

In 1845 the entire interior of the church was panelled, and a flat ceiling fitted. At the restoration in 1927–29 (undertaken by Georg Eliassen) this was removed, exposing the painted walls from the 17th century. The decoration in the extended nave has recently been completed by Arnstein Arneberg, basing himself on the fragment of a wall from the demolished stave church in Lårdal.

It has not been established whether this church, as might be expected for this type and this part of the country, had a narrower chancel and apse, or whether the chancel originally as well had the same width as the nave, as might be suggested by the pentice and various other details.

In 1845 the doorway is reported to have been moved from the south to the west wall. The present belfry is from 1727.

The church is dedicated to St. Nicholas of Bari, the miracle-working bishop of Lycia from about 350 AD. A small wooden sculpture (of which a copy is to be found in the church) was carried in procession every Midsummer's Day three times round the nearby lake, where it was immersed in the water as a sign of the forgiveness of sins.

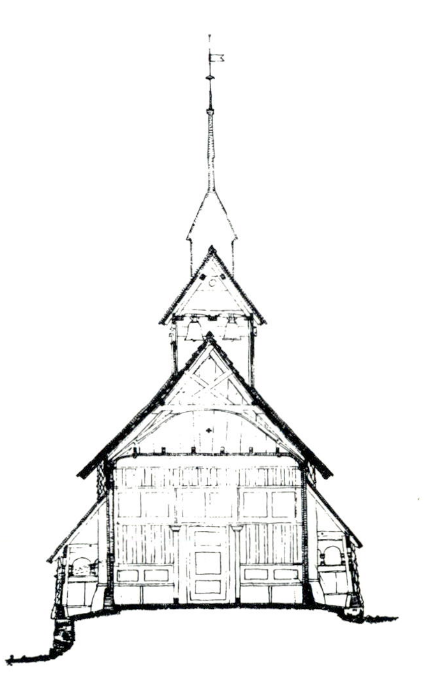

Eidsborg's exterior recalls to some extent its «bigger relations», the mast churches, but free masts and a raised central portion are lacking. The pentice has no structural significance.

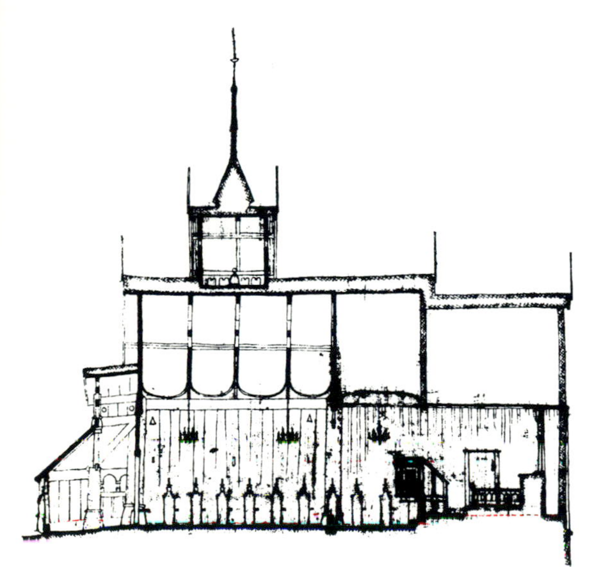

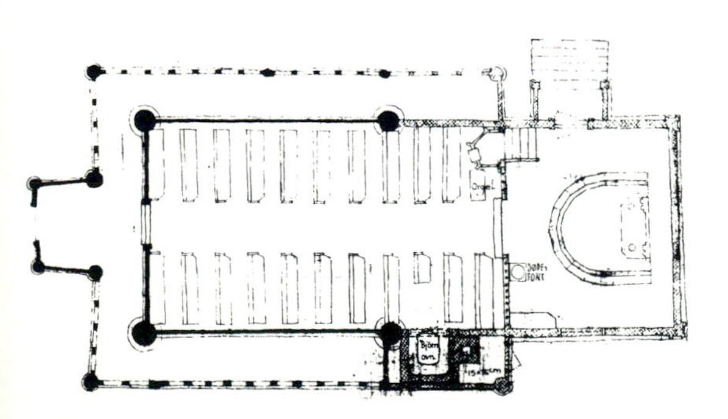

7. GRIP

This church, believed to have been built in the 15th century, still preserves its mediaeval core. The wall planking was replaced in 1621, and shortly afterwards decoratively painted. New windows were inserted in the 1870s, and the inner and outer walls panelled and painted white.

In 1933 a comprehensive programme of restoration was undertaken. The building was raised and placed on new foundations, the outer walls were repanelled and tarred, and the decorated interior panel once again brought to light. Some of the more recent window apertures were blocked up. The present ones are believed to correspond with those of the 17th century. A triptych from the Middle Ages, belived to be of Dutch origin, was reinstated.

The nave and chancel have the same width (12 x 6.5 m), which in parallel cases is generally due to subsequent rebuilding. The bearing mediaevel skeleton of sills and cornerposts is in this case supplemented by intermediate posts in the longitudinal walls. The saddle roof supports a belfry at the west end.

The authorities have recently advised against carrying out a suggestion that Grip Church should be moved to the mainland. It is recommended that until further notice it should be used as the local church, until such time as the conservation plan submitted for preserving the island's wooden buildings has been adopted.

Triptych from the Middle Ages, probably of Dutch origin.

The medieval post construction appears in the plan drawing.

Below: Row of houses («gata») on the island of Grip. South-east facade. (Vidar Sandbak Edvardsen)

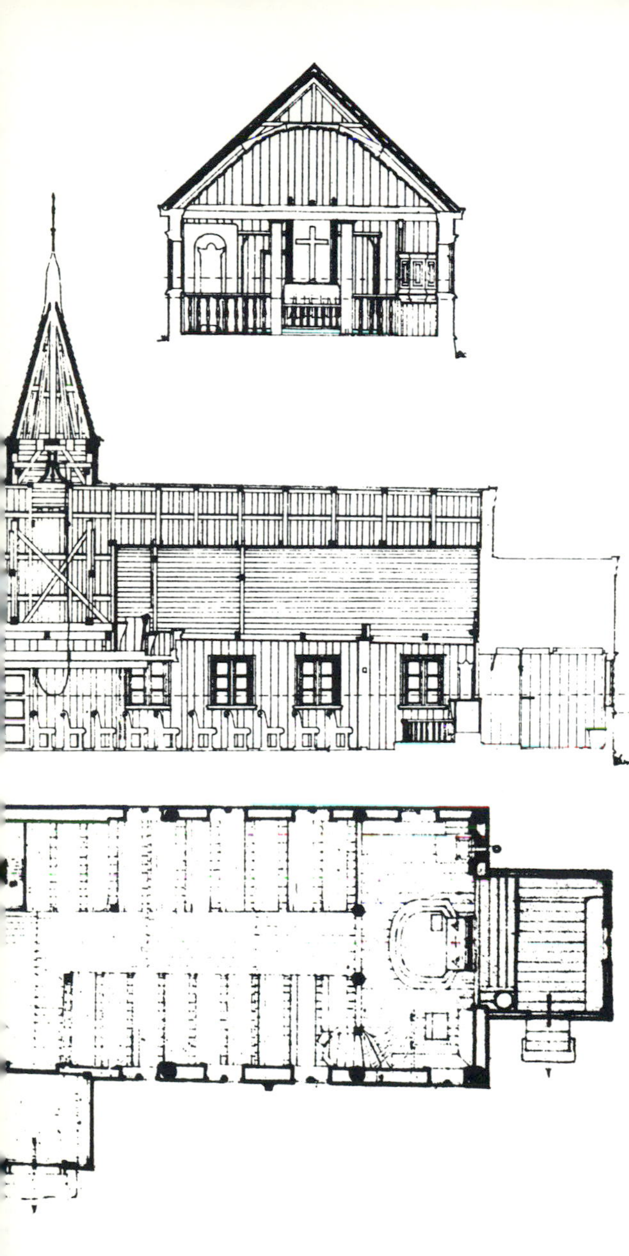

8. RØDVEN

The outer walls of the nave, with round cornerposts and intermediate posts, sills, and planking with the usual interior edge mouldings, are all from the Middle Ages.

The chancel now has the same width as the nave, although originally it was narrower. The two round posts in the rood screen were originally cornerposts for the former chancel, and indicate its width. The present one has square-cut posts and panelling of hewn plank, with a different, outside moulding, which suggests a date around the 17th century.

The mediaeval church was entirely surrounded by pentices, which were pulled down in connection with the rebuilding of the chancel. At the same time the outer walls were panelled, and the small leaded windows probably inserted.

It has not been definitely established whether the unusual external diagonal props («skorder») were added at the time, or whether they belonged to the original building. In the stave church context they appear primitive, nor were they structurally necessary as long as the pentices and the mediaeval roofing were still intact.

The log-built vestry to the north of the chancel was erected in 1651. In 1712 Hans Kundsen of Molde was commissioned by the local pastor, Thomas von Westen, to build the porch in the west. The roof and belfry then acquired their present shape. Ceiling (subsequently renovated), pulpit, altar, and altar panels have also been ascribed to him. The large lower windows are believed to have been inserted in 1824.

The Gothic stylistic features of the south entrance enable us to assign a date to it, and consequently the church, of about 1300. The north door, and probably the two posts in the rood-screen, as well as about one-third of the wall planks, were probably part of an older church, which may have been built on this site towards the end of the 12th century.

The large crucifix is from the 13th century. The rood-screen was erected in connection with the extension of the chancel in the 17th century, but contains ornamented mediaeval parts.

The style of the internal wall paintings would indicate a date around the 17th century (see also *Kvernes*).

Right: Sectional drawing of the chancel with cross section. The middle posts are corner posts in the original chancel. (H. Christie)

Below: the diagonal props supporting the building correspond with the intermediate posts in the walls.

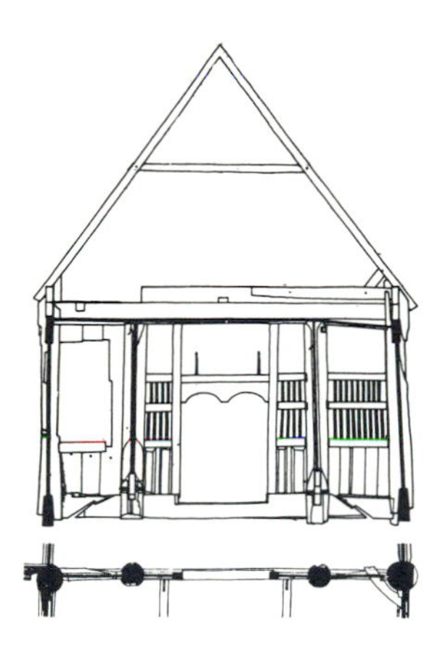

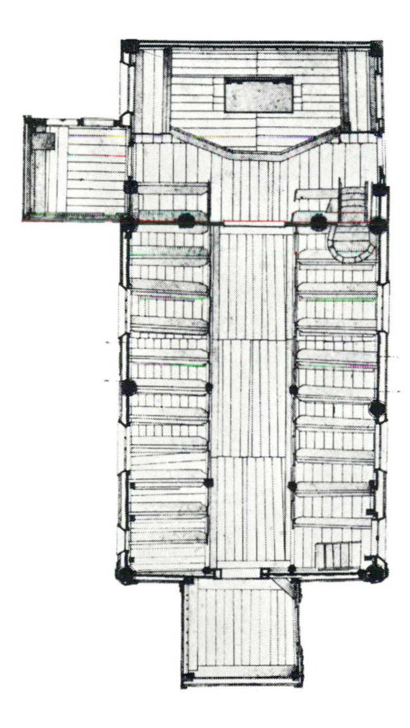

9. KVERNES

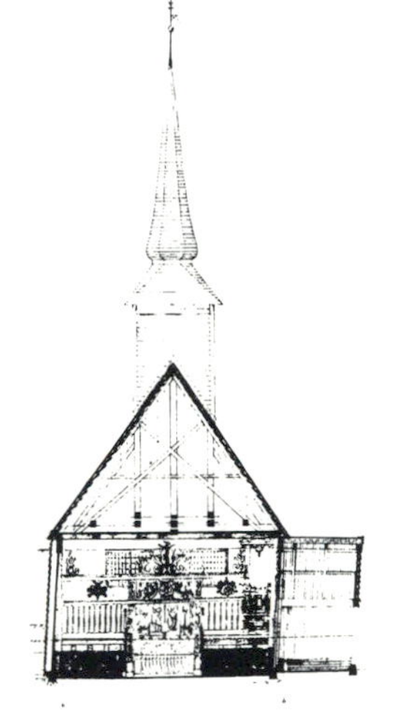

The shape of this church, with the nave and chancel of the same width, the exterior, with the characteristic props, all add up to a considerable similarity with Rødven.

However, the nave measures as much as 7.5 x 16 m, as against Rødven's 6.5 x 9 m. For this reason the mediaeval frame in Kvernes shows as much as three intermediate posts in the long walls, and two in the west wall.

Apart from this, there is little we know about the church's mediaeval shape, or the year it was built, as it has never been investigated archaeologically. It is mentioned in Aslak Bolt's rent roll in about 1432.

In 1633 the original chancel was pulled down and the present one erected in notched log technique. At the same time a stave-built baptistry was erected at the west end of the church, using wall planking that may derive from the original chancel.

It is probable that on that occasion the main entrance was moved from the west to the south. Both this and the south entrance to the chancel are devoid of any decor that could provide a basis for dating.

The vestry and porch in front of the entrance to the chancel are believed to have been added about 1670.

The cost of the lavishly adorned interior dating back to 1633 was largely defrayed by the incumbent, Anders Ericksen, as recorded on a tablet.

The interior decor of the nave differs from that in the chancel, and is considered the work of the same craftsman as in Rødven (Johan Kontrafeier, c. 1640).

In the middle of the church stands a post supporting the belfry. It is of later date, and has not been incorporated in the same way into the main construction as in other central mast churches known to us. In fact, up to the year 1899, when repairs were undertaken, it was asymmetrically placed, in connection with a gallery. The minister's chair was situated above the entrance to the baptistry at the west end.

The nave with the three intermediate posts in the longitudinal walls are from the Middle Ages, the timbered chancel (same width) from 1633. The narrower chancel-like annex at the west end is the baptistry.

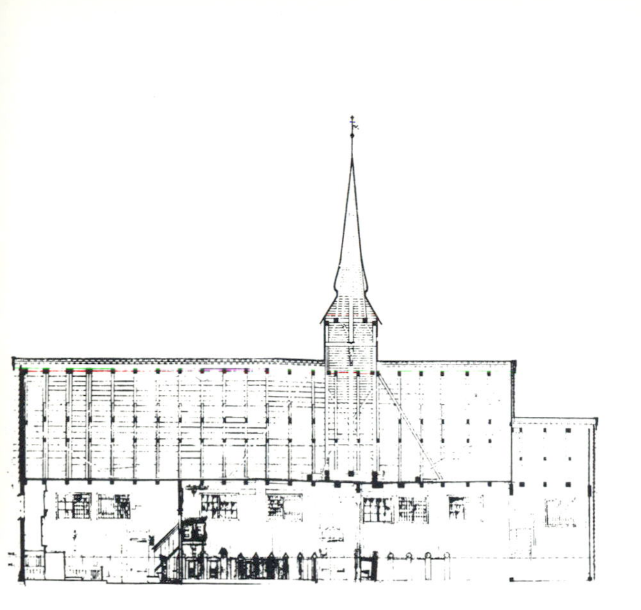

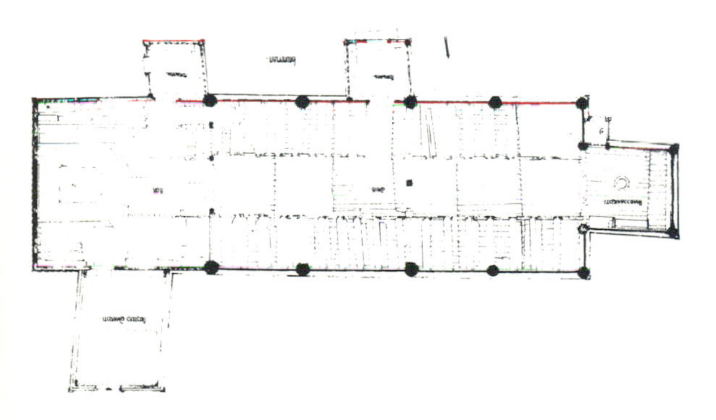

10. GARMO

The amateur antiquarian Anders Sandvig, creator of the Maihaugen Collection, considered that this, his find, derived from «the childhood of the stave church» in the days of St. Olav, round about 1020–30.

Although it is difficult to interprete the building history of this church, there is no firm basis for assigning a specially early date to it.

It was standing in the grounds of Garmo Farm in Vågå in 1882 when it was pulled down and its component parts scattered around.

With the aid of his local helpmeet Trond Eklestuen, Sandvig managed to collect most of them, and assisted by the architect Jürgensen re-erected the building in 1920 as a museum piece at Maihaugen, near Lillehammer.

Nave, chancel, and vestry are stave-built, and of the same width. The original chancel is assumed to have been narrower, and possibly to have had an apse. The longitudinal walls of the nave have an intermediate post; beyond this, and all the way to the chancel, the wall planking has been removed and used afresh in the vestry, with new posts. The notched log wings were added to the nave.

On the basis of church accounts Sandvig was able to assign a date of 1690 to this main conversion, as well as the tower and the porch. He believed that previously the church had possessed a pentice.

The roofing and tower in their present state go back to 1920.

The half columns flanking the main entrance and the door to the vestry, the church's galleries, and the oldest leaded windows can also, according to Sandvig, be ascribed to the main conversion of 1690. Various items of inventory have been taken from other churches in the valley.

The sketches on the left (Ole Øvergaard) show the three assumed stages of development, the last from 1690.

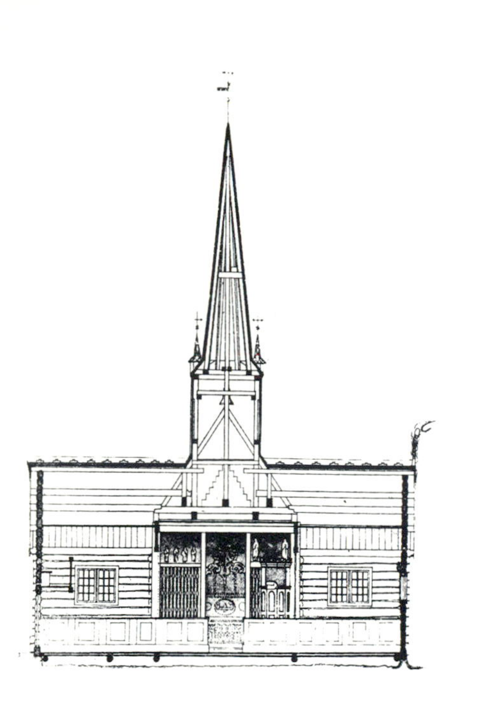

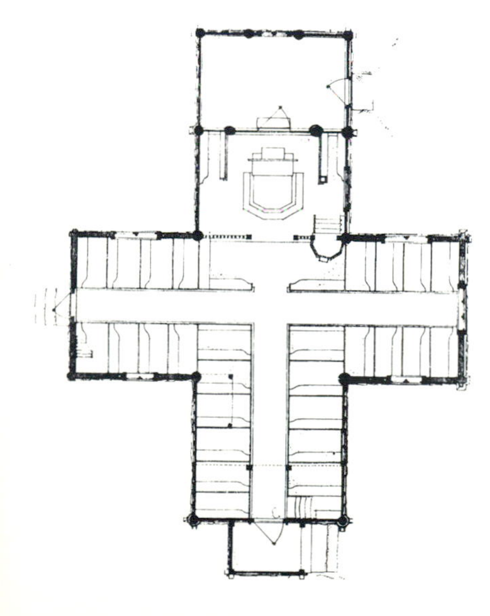

11. RØLDAL

The fame of this church may primarily be ascribed to the miraculous crucifix from the mid-13th century, and the lavish ornamentation of the interior.

The architect Jens Z. Kielland investigated this church in 1902 and supervised its restoration in 1917, with Domenico Erdmann as his consultant on matters of colour.

At that time the church was panelled, and painted both outside and inside. Careful examination showed that the mediaeval walls of the nave had been preserved, with round cornerposts and inserted square-hewn intermediate posts. These rest direct on the stone foundation, with sill beams morticed inbetween, whereas posts as a general rule ride over the sill beams and their point of intersection. This ensures a more stable structure.

Kielland assumes that the original church was built without a chancel, but that one was added as far back as the Middle Ages. He believes that the wall planking removed for the chancel arch is now to be found in the chancel wall.

He also holds the view that the church had a flagstone floor, and that there is evidence of a ceiling supported by six beams, as well as pentices.

Repairs carried out in 1844 involved increasing the height of the church by the addition of two rounds of logs, and installing a flat ceiling as well as a new roof construction. At the same time the nave was extended to the west, where planks from the original west wall can now be seen. The gallery was moved, and a tower erected.

Presumably on this occasion the church was also panelled. The old exquisitely carved pews with their doors were retained.

The wall decorations in the nave and chancel, uncovered and exhaustively restored by Erdmann, can be assigned to the late 1600s. The chancel ceiling was decorated in 1638.

The soapstone font is from the 13th century, while the pulpit and altar panels were painted by Gotfrid Hendtzcell in 1629.

Despite vigorous and repeated official protests belief in the miraculous powers of the crucifix persisted into the 19th century.

The mediaeval parts of the church are shown in full-drawn line.

Crucifix from the 1200s.

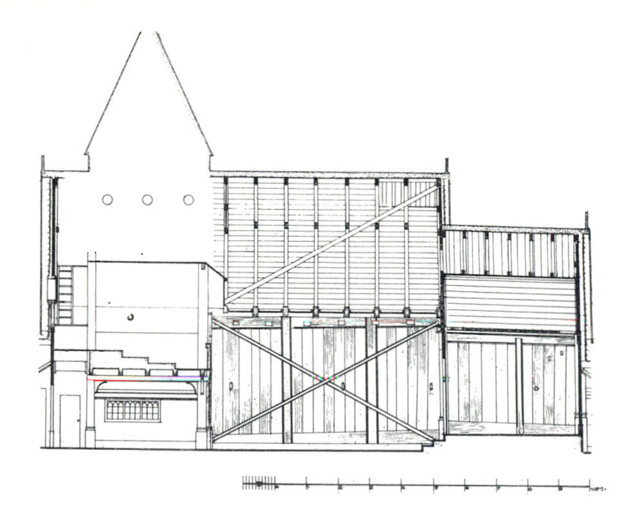

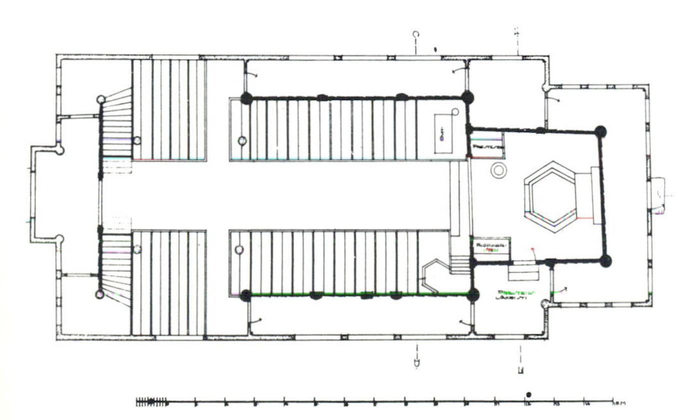

12. NORE

Apart from Uvdal, this is the only surviving church with a central mast. Today they are both cruciform; the striking feature of Nore is that it acquired its cruciform design as far back as the Middle Ages.

In its original guise, too, Nore was very similar to Uvdal: a stave-built nave with a narrower chancel, terminating in an apse, with a pentice running right round, and a belfry supported by the central mast. This is buttressed both against the upper bressummer and a pair of rafters, no doubt a necessity since the bells were suspended in the belfry. A freestanding bell-tower, or steeple, forming an extension at the west end, is known to us from other stave churches. In such cases the purely decorative belfry then merely rests on the rafter construction. At its foot the central mast is morticed into the cross raft beam of a ground frame (cf. the mast churches). In Nore the central mast is intact, while the belfry was replaced in 1730.

Shortly after being built the church acquired stave-built wings. Traces for planks in the intermediate posts of the longitudinal walls indicate the width, while the height was the same as in the nave. There is convincing evidence that the wings, in common with the chancel, had an *apse,* possibly with a perivalium (conical roof surmounted by a round turret, as, for example, at Borgund). This discovery of his justified Dr Anders Bugge in describing the church as «a unique example of a stave church».

The *present* log built transepts were added early in the 1700s, together with galleries, of which one was also installed above the west end of the nave.

In other respects the nave has retained its mediaeval form, apart from the ceiling. The chancel was rebuilt and extended in 1683 in stave construction, partly deriving from the former chancel, and given the same width and practically the same length as the nave. A log porch and vestry are from 1723 and 1753 respectively, while a date around 1200 has been assigned to the west door.

The oldest decorations in the church date back to 1655 and were carried out at the same time and by the same painter as at Uvdal (q.v.).

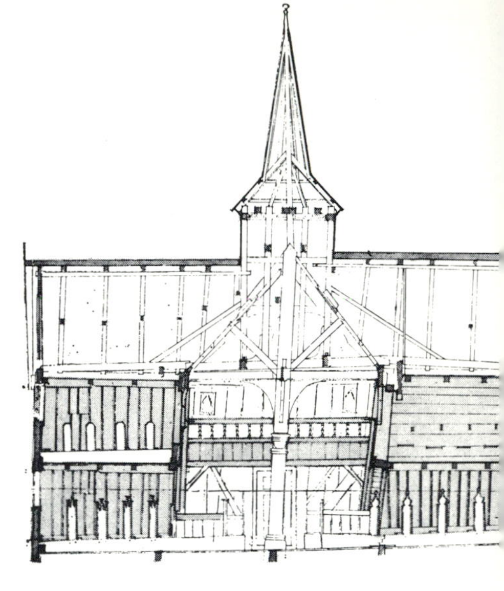

Traces indicate a former lecturing gallery in eastern part of nave.

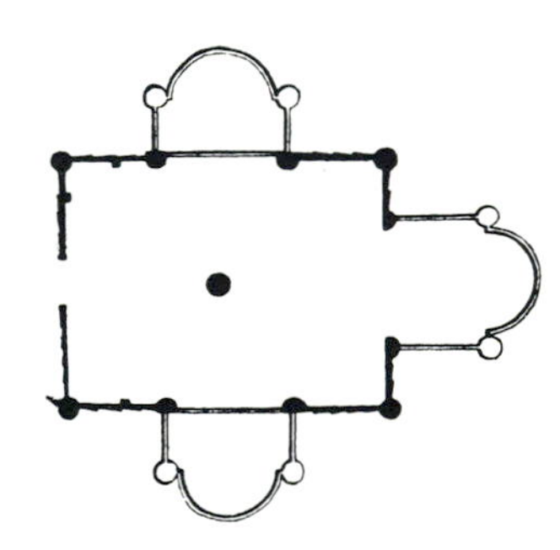

The mediaeval chancel and wings terminating in apses (A. Bugge). (See *Kalundborg,* p. 7.)
Sectional drawing showing how the mast is buttressed (cp. Reinli). (Anders Bugge)

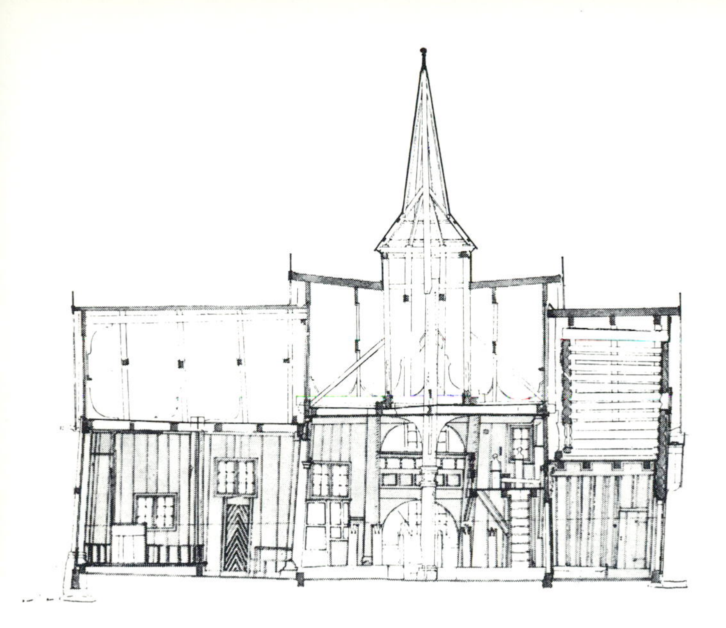

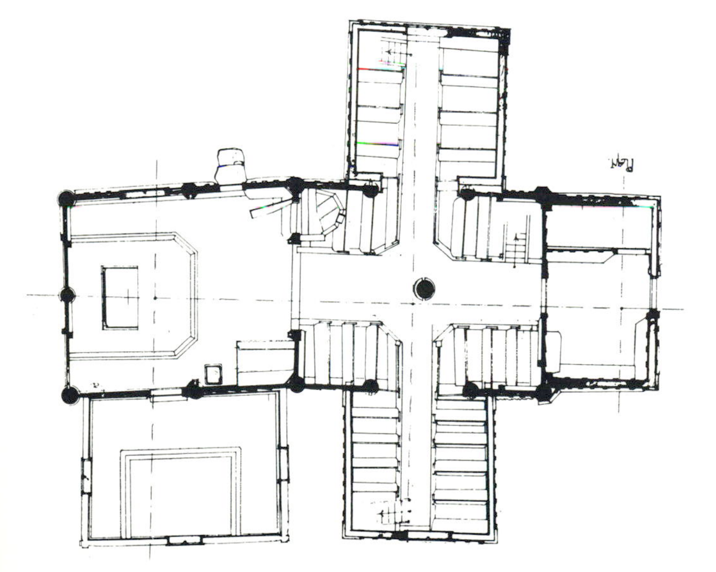

13. UVDAL

Like its nearby «relative» at Nore, this church contains lavish 17th-century wall-painting. Tendrils and roses – a common decorative feature of Norwegian vernacular architecture – spread gaily and irreverently across structural features and supplementary details. The congregation could in truth enjoy the glow of this exuberant wealth of colour; at the same time the almost chaotic effect of the many complicated architectural intrusions is mitigated, so that the entire interior presents a harmonious and charming whole.

Only the front part of the nave, with the polygonal cross section central mast, which supported the belfry and worked in constructively with the walls, roof structure and ground frame (see *Nore,* and *Nes,* p. 15), is part of the original building. The church had a narrower chancel with an apse, and a pentice running all the way round.

Shortly after building the nave was extended 3.5 m. to the west, in full width and height. The west wall was moved and given a new doorway. In its former place, a central mast with a clover-leaf cross-section was introduced. Together with the first mast this may have been necessary in order to support a new belfry.

The chancel, too, was extended in the Middle Ages, and the apse demolished. The apse arch (now a picture-frame) can still be seen, although the chancel was once again extended in 1684, on this occasion in the entire width of the church. The previous width of the chancel is indicated by the original corner-posts, which now flank the chancel opening; the chancel arch is also preserved. The south door of the old chancel was fitted into the new one. The oldest decorations are from 1656, when a ceiling was installed in the nave and chancel.

In 1720 the church acquired more or less its present appearance, stave-built wings being added in the middle of the longitudinal walls of the nave, both with galleries. The porch was erected at the west end, and a new belfry put up, supported by the two central masts. The oldest of these ends at the same height as the roof ridge, the more recent one at the ceiling.

Finally, in about 1800 a log-work vestry was added at the north end of the chancel.

The banisters, with their 14th century carvings, in the gallery above the western annexe of the nave, have, on the basis of evidence that has come to light, been part of a lecture gallery (see *Torpo*) in front of the chancel arch. The installation of this gallery may have necessitated the extension of the nave.

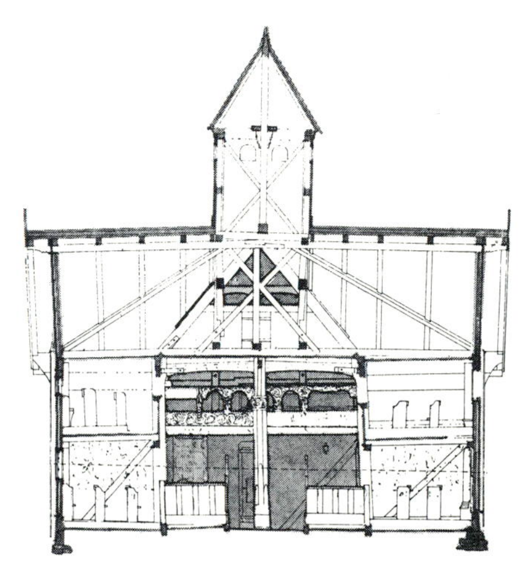

Opp. page:
Longitudinal section: The central mast to the left supported the belfry originally. The one on the right (west) is of later date. The present belfry is supported by both.
Bottom: Extension towards west, and lecturing gallery. (H. Christie.)

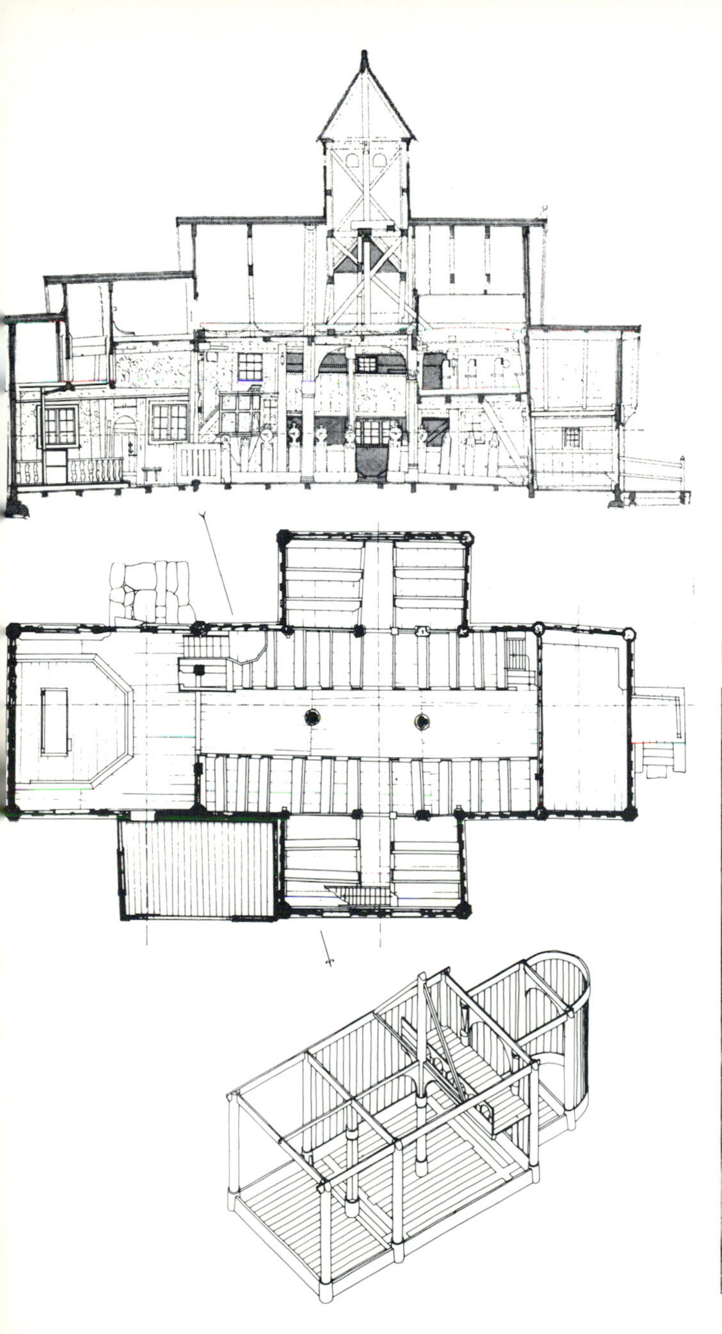

14. HØYJORD

This church was «discovered» behind external and internal panelling in 1904. The work of uncovering in the following year showed that the mediaeval walls with posts, intermediate posts, sills, and planking had been preserved, although greatly hacked about when the panelling was installed. The difference between the edge profile of the planking in the nave and chancel suggests that the latter is older.

The pentice was pulled down in 1689, when the roof structure was renovated and the exterior panelled. Among the material ordered at that time we find «one mast for the tower, 24 ells long, 8-inch top», measurements that might suggest a central mast. It would have proved a valuable addition for buttressing in a church of this size, where the links between posts and bressummers are not of the best.

The 1905 survey failed to reveal the existence of the central mast. It may not have been set up in 1689, as it may have proved superfluous when the flat, rigid ceiling was installed.

In 1953 the church was reopened after a restoration more exhaustive than would be envisaged today, under the supervision of the architect Otto Scheen.

Everything except the outer walls was pulled down, the latter being raised and placed on new foundations. The foundation stone for a central mast was dicovered, and one was erected, connected with the wall bressumers and bottom sills by means of beams. A new roof structure with shingle roofing, and a steeper pitch, was installed. This, and the new belfry, rest on the central mast, and on new, insulated external walls.

Inside, the mediaeval wall is to be found, with the original ogive and clover leaf-shaped squints. The decor was touched up, and a new arched vaulted ceiling installed in the chancel, on the basis of marks that were discovered. The oldest post-Reformation windows were reopened.

Traces of an original chancel rood-screen were insufficient to be restored. A new gallery was installed at the west end. The old doors were supplemented by new ones of the same kind, and an original south door in the nave was left blocked up.

The porch was renewed, with an open pentice. The vestry added at the turn of the last century was replaced by a new one «in harmony with the church's exterior».

The plan drawing (bottom next page) shows the medieval sections discovered in 1904. The central mast is missing. Centre: Present plan. Below: Original south wall in the nave, with middle-age light openings.

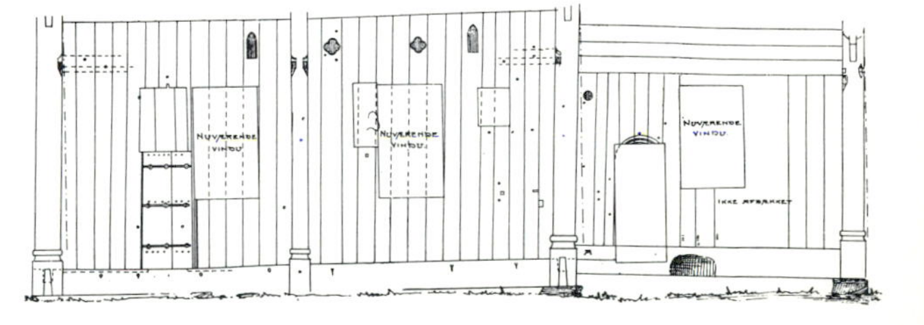

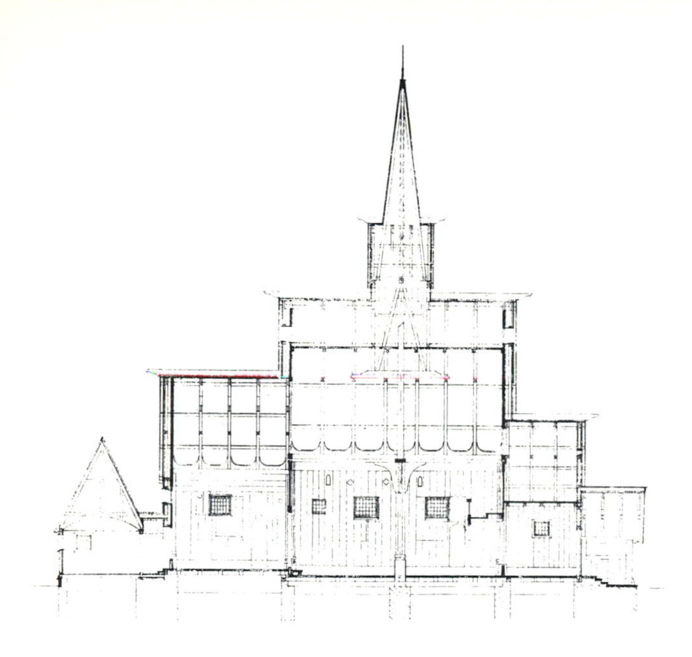

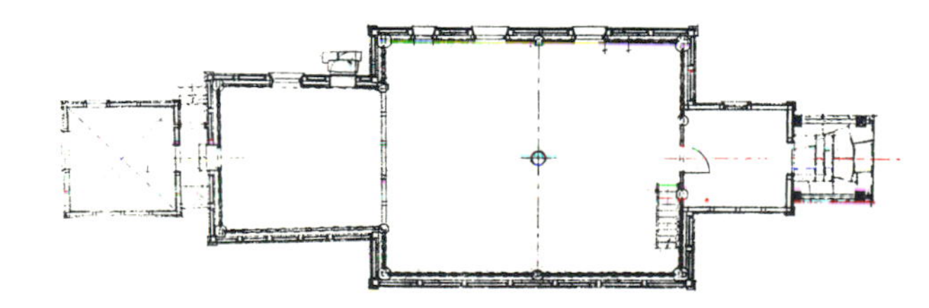

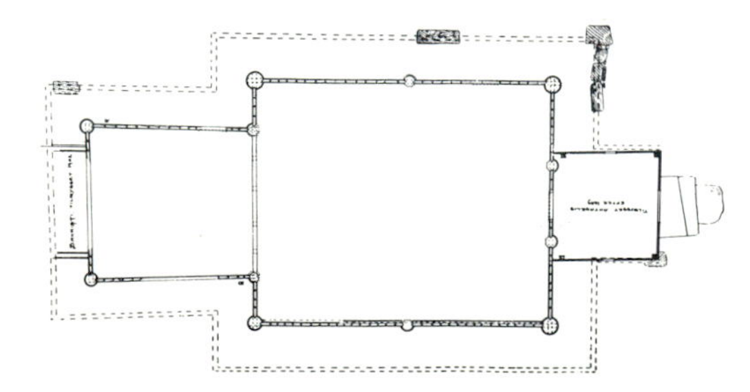

15. ØYE

The stave church was pulled down in 1747, when a log-built church was erected just across the road. Two hundred years later some of the old timbers were discovered under the church floor, in sufficient quantities to enable the stave church to be re-erected in 1960-65 with a reasonable degree of accuracy. The work was supervised by Cato Enger, building consultant to the Director of Ancient Monuments.

From the outside the church looks very much like a stave church of the single-nave type, with a pentice around the nave, chancel, and apse. It is therefore surprising to discover *four free masts* inside. These do not, as usual in mast churches, penetrate the roofing in a raised central section; they are, however, placed close to the corners, as in Hurum–Lomen. Across the room they are braced with a broad string beam, which is supported underneath by complete arches between the masts, and console-shaped semi-arches against the top bressummer of the outer wall. Accordingly the traditional system of bracing arches and struts round the masts has been abandoned.

On top, the masts run without further attachment directly into the roofing, which has been renovated. We are, in fact, dealing with a «single-nave mast church», a genuine exception to the general pattern, and a parallel to the demolished stave church from the neighbouring district of Vang. The survey of the latter (demolished in 1841), however, shows masts placed closer to the middle, dividing the sanctuary into nine equally large squares. (Excavations carried out beneath Urnes Church suggest a similar position for four earthed masts in an earlier church.) In Vang Church the masts were linked and terminated as in Øye, only by whole arches to the bressummer of the outer wall. The use of the masts may have been secondary (Arne Berg, 1979).

Øye Church poses a number of problems: the amputated keyhole-shaped door (replica *in situ*) suggests that the church was converted. The masts may have passed through the roof as supports for a raised central portion, with an unorthodox form of bracing, actually more like what is to be found in the central mast churches (Nes). As in these, the masts may also have supported or been part of the belfry, in a similar stabilising interaction with the outer walls. It is possible, however, that the motive was merely a desire to retain the four-mast tradition in Valdres.

Masts and cornerposts, and portions of the outer walls, are all original, as is the rood-screen with the narrow chancel arch and ogive openings, as well as the arched opening into the apse.

Bottom opp. page: the medieval portions during reconstruction in the 1960s. Below: Vang stave church undergoing demolition (moved in 1841 to the Riesengebirge).

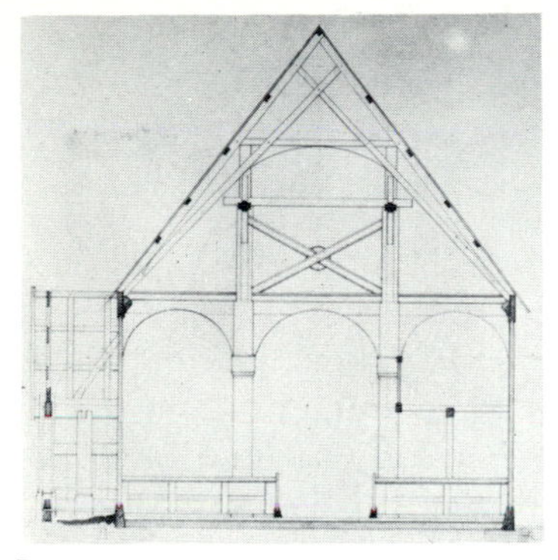

Vang

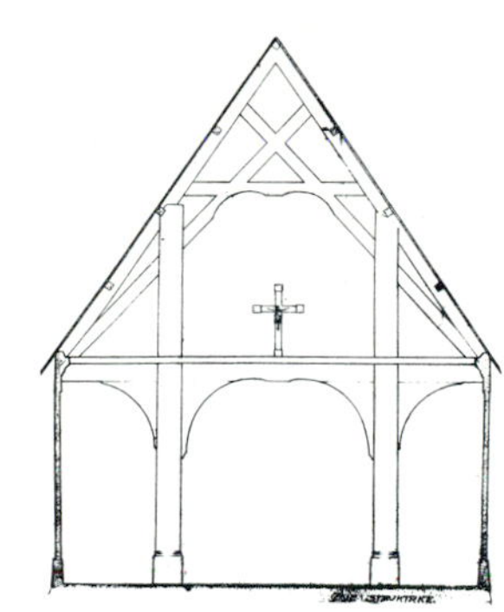

Øye

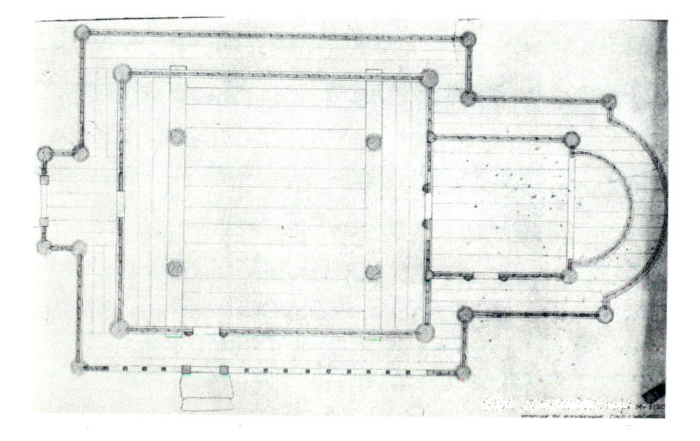

16. KAUPANGER

Unlike the mast churches of the Borgund group, all those in the Kaupanger group were built with all «free» masts on the longitudinal sides running right down to the floor, without (originally) any use of string beams and cross-braces. Towards the chancel, and the entrance, the middle mast has been truncated, and rests on an arch. This, together with the unbroken row of masts in the longitudinal walls, emphasizes the east–west axis, giving the interior the «basilical» appearance characteristic of this group.

In Kaupanger this is further accentuated by an extension of the nave, already in the Middle Ages. The four masts of the west front, together with the west wall, were moved out, and two new masts inserted in the longitudinal walls.

The uninterrupted tall masts, devoid of any decor apart from the moulded splays towards the top, give the Kaupanger church a certain Gothic air, as opposed to the Romanesque appearance of the rest in the group. Consequently, the flat raftered ceiling in the nave, installed as far back as early 17th century, represents an anticlimax.

The open row of masts provides an excellent opportunity for studying sophisticated structural details. Particularly striking in this case is the system of «internal flying buttresses», struts, beneath the roof of the ambulatory, which on all sides connects the masts to the bressummer in the outer walls, to which the struts are fixed. They comprise an indispensable part of the bracing in all mast churches, while at the same time contributing, with their graceful interconnected arch links, to enhance the spatial effect.

It will be seen that the chancel in principle is constructed like the nave, with two free masts running down to the floor, an ambulatory around them, a raised central portion, and an open scissor-braced roof structure. The masts have the same system of struts as in the nave, but the intermediate masts in the chancel are cut short, and rest on arches suspended from the upper bressummer of the openwork wall in the nave. Obviously the master builder met with problems when linking up the chancel with the outer wall of the nave. The solution varies from one church to another: masts running down to the floor are a feature of the Kaupanger group, while in the Borgund group they are usually cut short and suspended aloft, so that struts are not used.

The Kaupanger church was rebuilt in the 17th century and – somewhat infelicitously – in 1882.

An exhaustive restoration, completed in 1965 under the supervision of the architect Kristian Bjerknes, substantially recreated the church as it appeared in the 17th century. Excavations beneath the floor revealed traces of two earlier churches, both with earthed posts, and outer walls resting on sill beams.

The interior shows how the tall masts are braced against the outer wall. The system is particularly effective at the corner masts.
Longitudinal section shows the layer of beams in the nave and the medieval roof truss in the chancel.

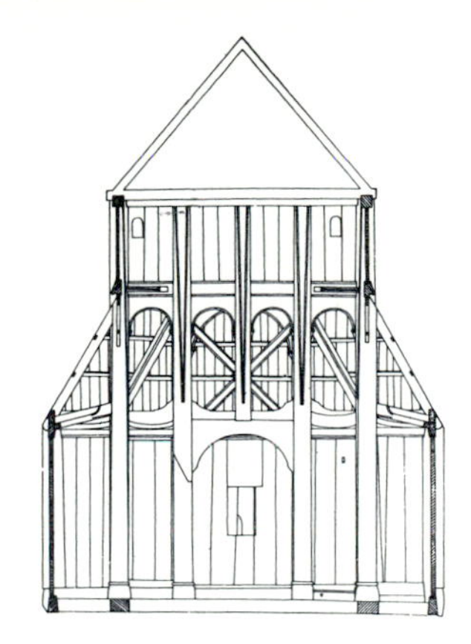

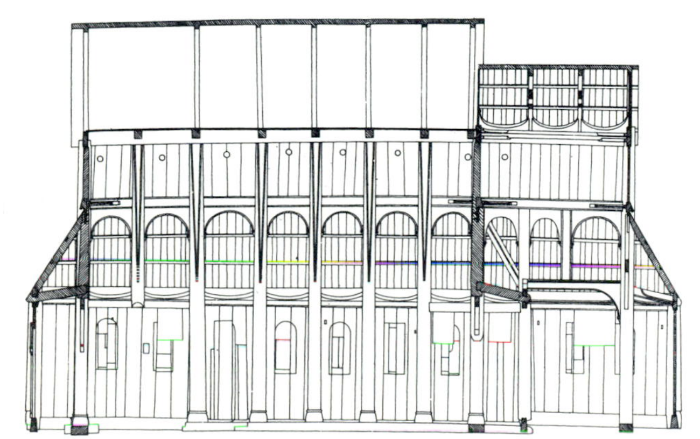

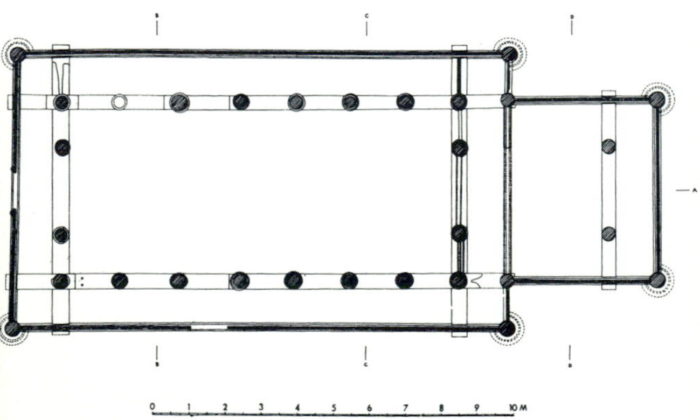
0 1 2 3 4 5 6 7 8 9 10 M

17. URNES

While in the Kaupanger church we are dealing with *masts*, in Urnes an attempt was made to recreate the *colonnade* of the Romanesque pillared basilica.

In their original version both of them had more or less the same plan: six masts along the longitudinal walls, all running down to the floor at equal distances; along the short sides five, the middle mast resting on an arch, in fact a basilical emphasis on the east-west axis. In both types the chancel has two free masts running down to the floor, but the Urnes chancel lacks intermediate masts as found in Kaupanger Church.

However, in Kaupanger the attributes are restricted to what is structurally necessary: inset quadrant brackets allowing the masts to run freely, and a system of struts surrounding them like a girdle. Urnes, on the other hand, in common with Hopperstad, has markedly moulded archivolts and decorated *capitals*, which visually divide the masts into a lower column and an upper pilaster. Similar decoration appears in the splay of the latter. In neither church do we find masks at the top of the masts.

The «triforium» effect produced by cross-braces and string beams in churches of the Borgund Type is abandoned. In the latter these elements are necessary to provide stability, since not all the masts go right down to the floor. In Hopperstad, presumably in Lom, too, and when Fortun Church was re-erected at Fantoft, these elements were added later, for safety's sake.

The chancel probably had an apse. The present stave-built rectangular extension was added in about 1600. The belfry was put up in 1704. The arcade in the west must be regarded as a remnant of a former – but not original – pentice that ran right round the church. – Installing the Munthe family pew in the 17th century involved cutting two masts, and necessitated the eye-soring cross-braces. In other respects the interior is characteristic of that period. – Inventory includes two Limoges candlesticks, and a mediaeval wroughtiron chandelier.

Urnes owns much of its reputation to the decorated portions of the north wall, and gables. These have no connection with the rest of the decor, having been part of an earlier church on the site, – with outer walls approximately 80 cm higher.

Excavations under the floor reveal traces of one or possibly two previous churches. Post-holes in the ground suggest that the later had four free masts, and that the outer walls rested in part on sills inserted between earthed posts.

On the basis of its ornamentation Urnes is usually considered the oldest among Norway's surviving stave churches. But it does not follow that as a *type* it represents the earliest, if compared with its sober neighbour at Kaupanger or the churches of the Borgund group.

The doorway below was part of an earlier Urnes church, and was fitted into the north wall. The wood carving, with the emphasis on animal patterns, has given name to the Urnes style.

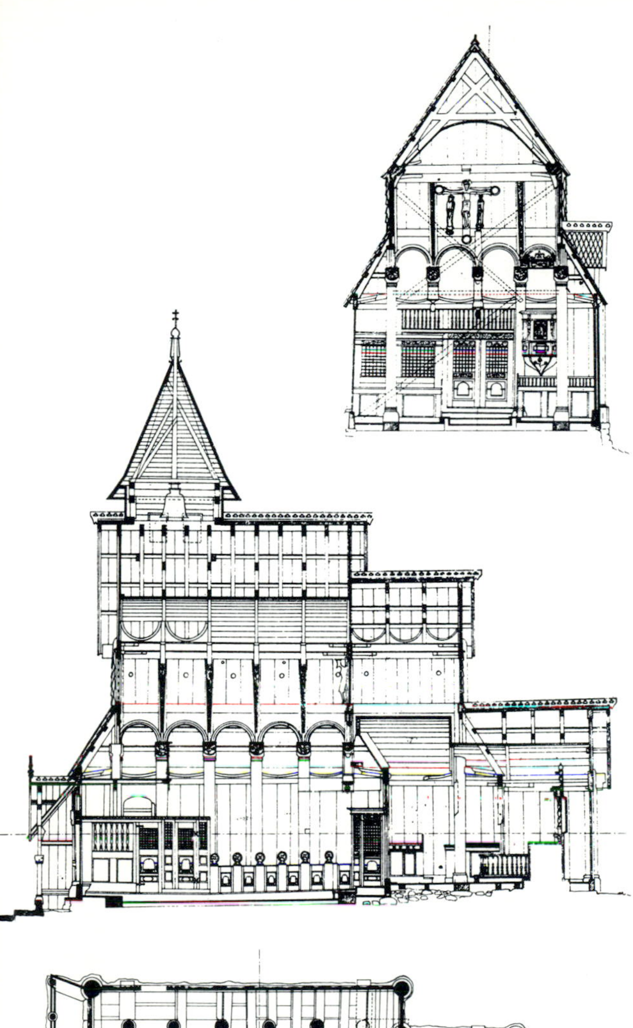

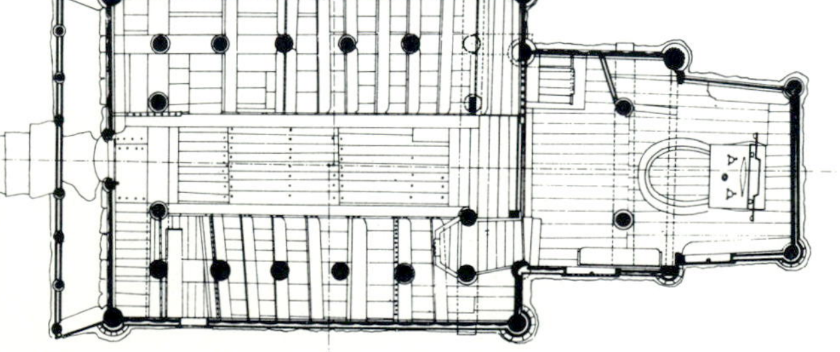

18. HOPPERSTAD

Here the similarity with Urnes can be traced element by element: the number of masts and their position in the nave and chancel, a structure without string beams and cross-braces, which in this case were added later in the Middle Ages. We can even recognise the archivolts and capitals from Urnes, although the decor there, and on the splays, is missing. The intention, recreating the continental basilica in wood, is the same, with reservations and limitations consequent on the demands and special conditions imposed by building in wood.

The church was saved from being pulled down in the 1880s thanks to the efforts of the architect Peter Blix, who, together with his antiquarian friend Nicolaysen, also supervised its restoration. As far as the exterior was concerned the Borgund church served as a model. Missing elements, such as the pentice, apse with tower, and belfry, were added, with some adjustments, mainly in ornamental details.

Of these, the robust semi-spherical bases of the cornerposts in the nave are particularly striking. While the west door, with its early animal ornamentation, had to be completed, the south door, with its purely architectural theme, was intact.

The interior had been well preserved, as well as the original rood screen with the round arched door; the shafts of its pillars are lined and braced at the bottom with brackets, in genuine stave-church fashion. The ogive wall apertures were adopted in Gothic times.

The canopy above the side altar is from the 14th century, with contemporary paintings. The interior had acquired painted wall decor in the 17th century, the bulk of which was removed during Blix's somewhat purist mediaeval restoration.

He left untouched, however, the cross-braces which thrust their way so forcefully into the capitals of the masts. The architect Kristian Bjerknes is responsible for the reconstructed version shown on this page, representing the original state (cf. Urnes).

Plan, cross section right: Kr. Bjerknes's reconstruction of the original medieval shape.

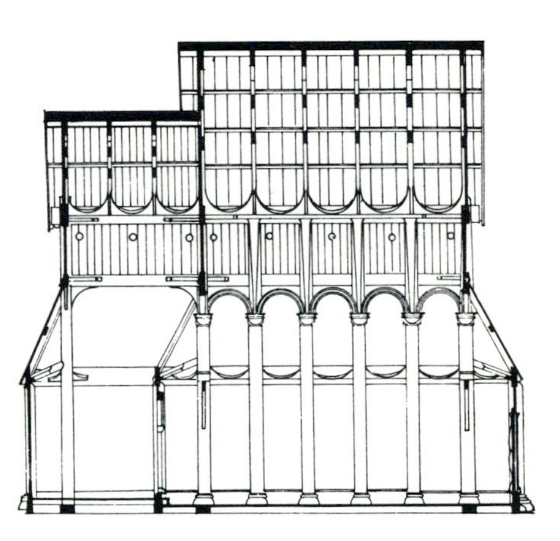

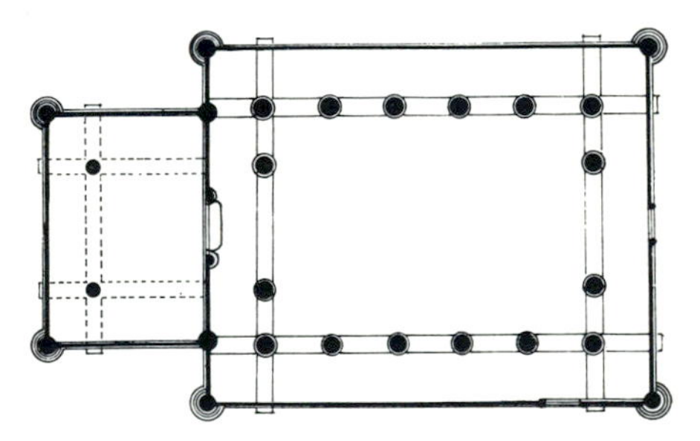

Plan, cross section opposite page: The church as it emerged in the 1880s after Blix's restoration, and as it appears today.

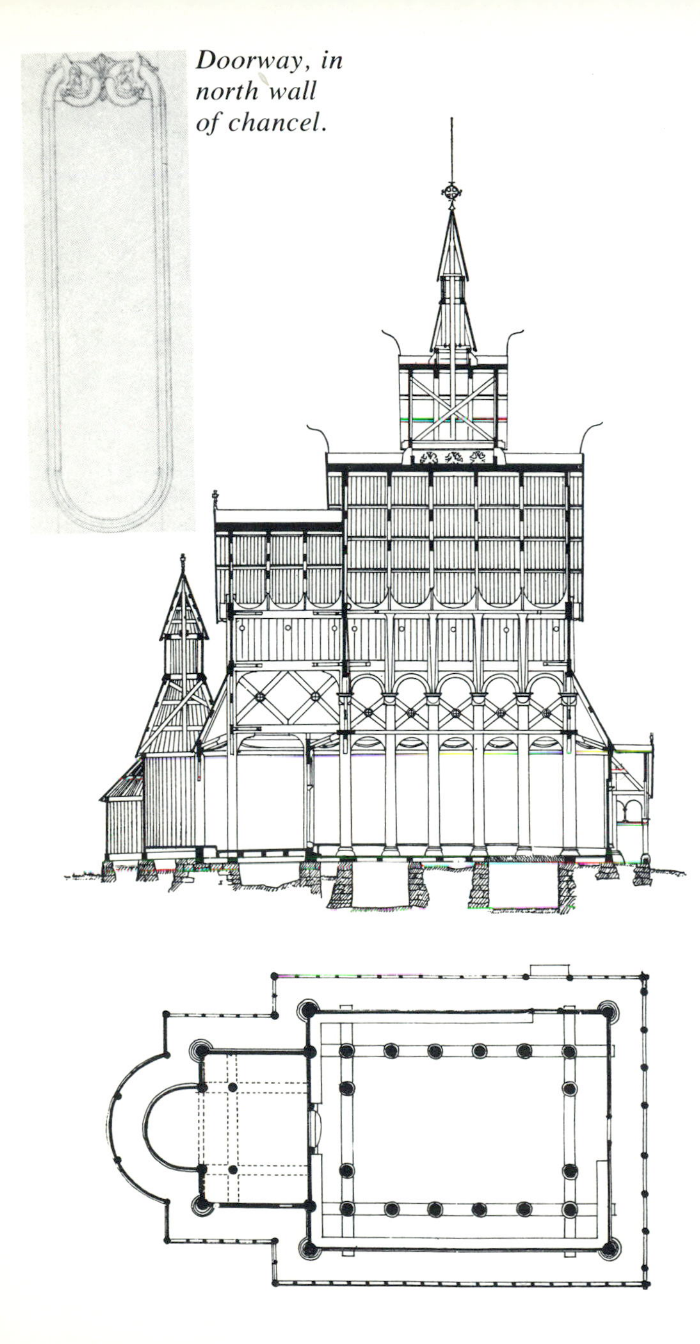

Doorway, in north wall of chancel.

19. FORTUN (Fantoft)

In the spring of 1883 the young antiquarian A. Lorange visited Fortun. He had been commissioned by his father-in-law, the consul Gade, to supervise the pulling down of a condemned stave church, and its removal to Gade's property at Fantoft, just outside Bergen.

A contemporary photograph reveals that at that time the church had panelled walls, a west tower, and timbered chancel, erected respectively in 1651 and 1666. The pentices had been removed.

After its transfer to Fantoft the church fetched external features such as a belfry, a chancel with an apse, and entrance gables from Borgund, while the open gallery with arcades was inspired by Urnes. Inside, the chancel acquired two free masts, and the nave rather unfelicitously fitted string beams with cross-braces, which were certainly not part of the original church. This complete «face-lift» was based partly on contemporary conception of the Middle Ages, and partly on good faith.

In 1940 the architect Kristian Bjerknes, with unerring logic, pointed out the mistakes made.

Lorange and his assistant Mathiesen assumed that, when the chancel was pulled down in 1666, use was made of its masts, trimmers, and arches in extending the nave westwards. Consequently, these parts were «put back» when reconstruction took place, and the nave was correspondingly shortened. Admittedly, measurements undertaken in 1854 by the architect G. Bull show that the double span of the Fantoft chancel was situated in the west end of the nave, but it cannot possibly have been *extended,* since the tower was in position there fifteen years before the chancel was replaced.

Bjerknes maintains that the structural elements in dispute were never in the chancel, nor were they parts of the *original* nave at all. The latter must have had seven masts, evenly spaced along the longitudinal walls, corresponding with the rafters. The double span could be ascribed to an alteration undertaken in 1656, when the church for the first time acquired galleries.

The chancel may be assumed to have had two free masts running down to the floor, but otherwise its original state is a matter of uncertainty.

Devoid of its present string beams, cross-braces and lower arches – an encroachment justified by analogous style studies – we should get a stave church closely akin to that at Kaupanger. With its unusually lofty, length-orientated nave Fortun had still more in common with Hafslo Church (pulled down in 1875, see page 16).

Fantoft Church is still privately owned, being the property of the shipowner Jacob Kjøde.

Below: Before demolition.

Sections: top, original condition, centre: rebuilt about 1656, bottom: the church as it was set up at Fantoft (Kr. Bjerknes).

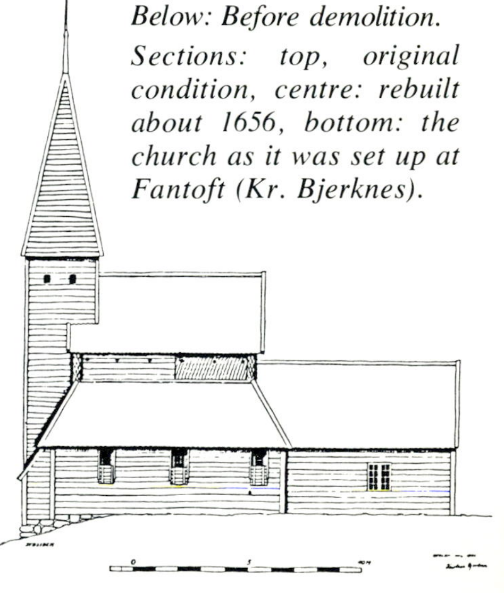

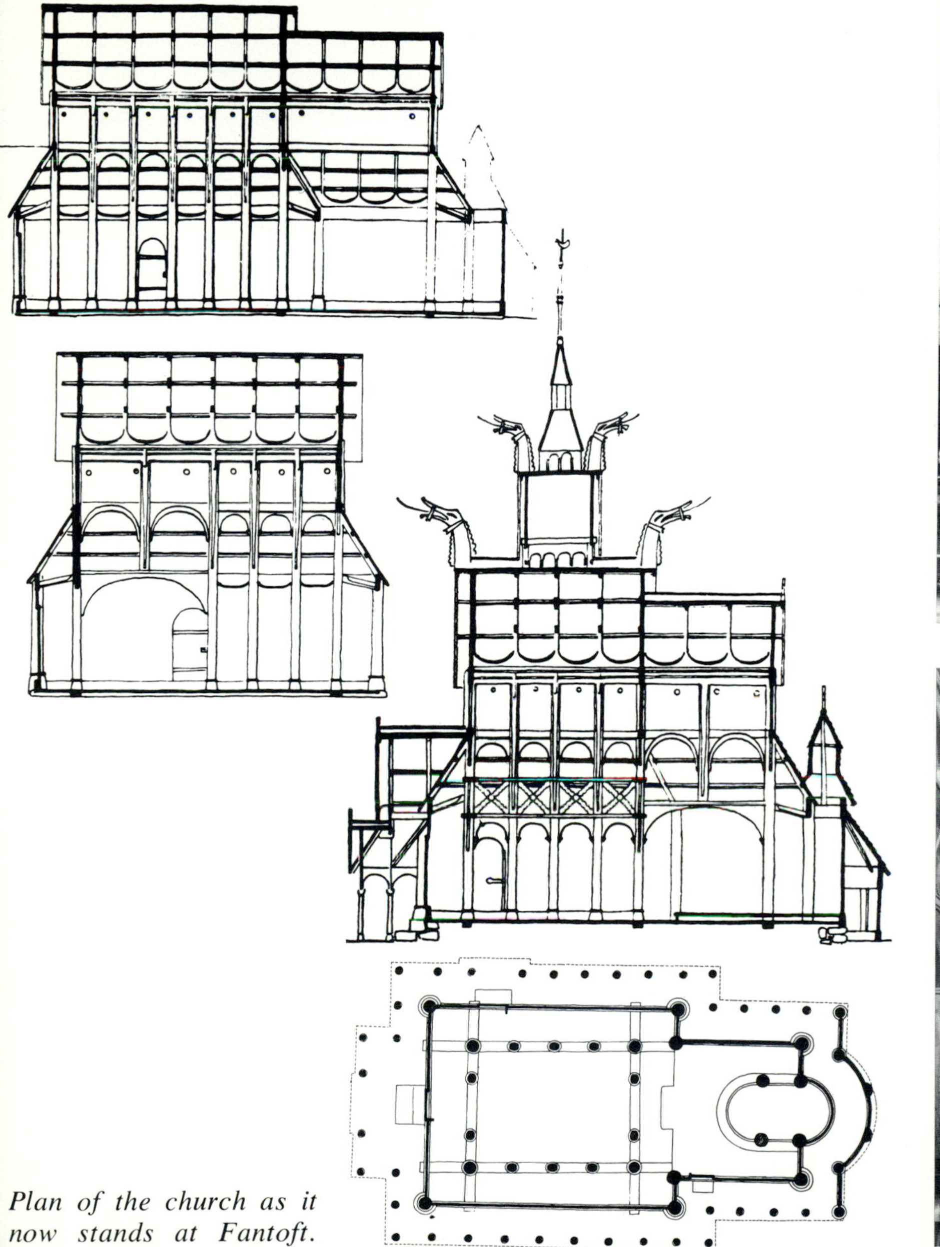

Plan of the church as it now stands at Fantoft.

20. LOM

This church owes its impressive appearance, the central tower with its spire and finials, to Werner Olsen, masterbuilder of the church at Vågå. At the same time (1663) he added wings in raised timbers, thus producing a cruciform church. The wings were somewhat lower than the nave, without a raised central section as in the nave and chancel.

This meant that the pentices had to be pulled down. Like the apse, these dated back to the Middle Ages, but were hardly original.

In 1634 the nave had acquired an extension in the west end, log-built. Compared to the graceful stave and raised timber work, the extension has the effect of a massive foreign element, and with its considerable height, equal to that of the nave, it has created technical problems by sagging. However, an extension of the interior perspective was achieved, in which the mediaeval stave-built core, with the eight masts on each side, still dominates the picturesque additions made to the church in subsequent ages.

The cross-section of the masts is elliptical right down to the bottom, with square-cut ends, so that a certain pierced arcade wall effect is achieved. One perceives the cruciform church, without the feeling of wholeness being forfeited.

The short sides of the nave have five masts, of which the middle one is truncated, and rests on the lower string beam, supported by an arch. The church is said to have been built without string beams and cross-braces, but these were installed shortly afterwards, probably in order to improve stability. With all the masts of the longitudinal sides running down to the floor, and the emphasis on the central axis, Lom must therefore be regarded as belonging to the «basilical» churches of the Kaupanger group.

When the tower was erected in 1663 it was decided to install a flat raftered ceiling in the nave. During the process of restoration in 1933 this was removed, revealing once again the mediaeval trussed rafters.

The pulpit and chancel arch executed in baroque scroll carving are the work of Jakob Sæterdalen.

The capping, crosses, and one of the gable dragons are the only ones to have survived from the Middle Ages (replicas *in situ*, originals at Maihaugen).

In the north wing stands a doorway which prior to rebuilding may have been the south door of the nave.

This church is still used as the local parish church.

Longitudinal section opposite page showing the medieval parts. Below: Traces of earthed posts below the church from an earlier stave church, presumably with detached masts inside. (H. Christie) See introduction (p. 18) and development diagram.

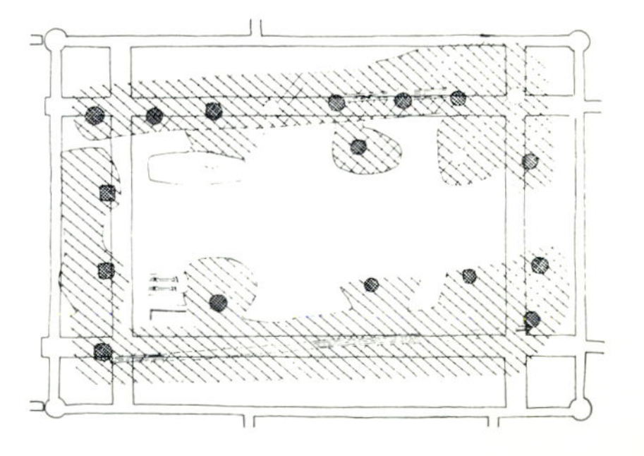

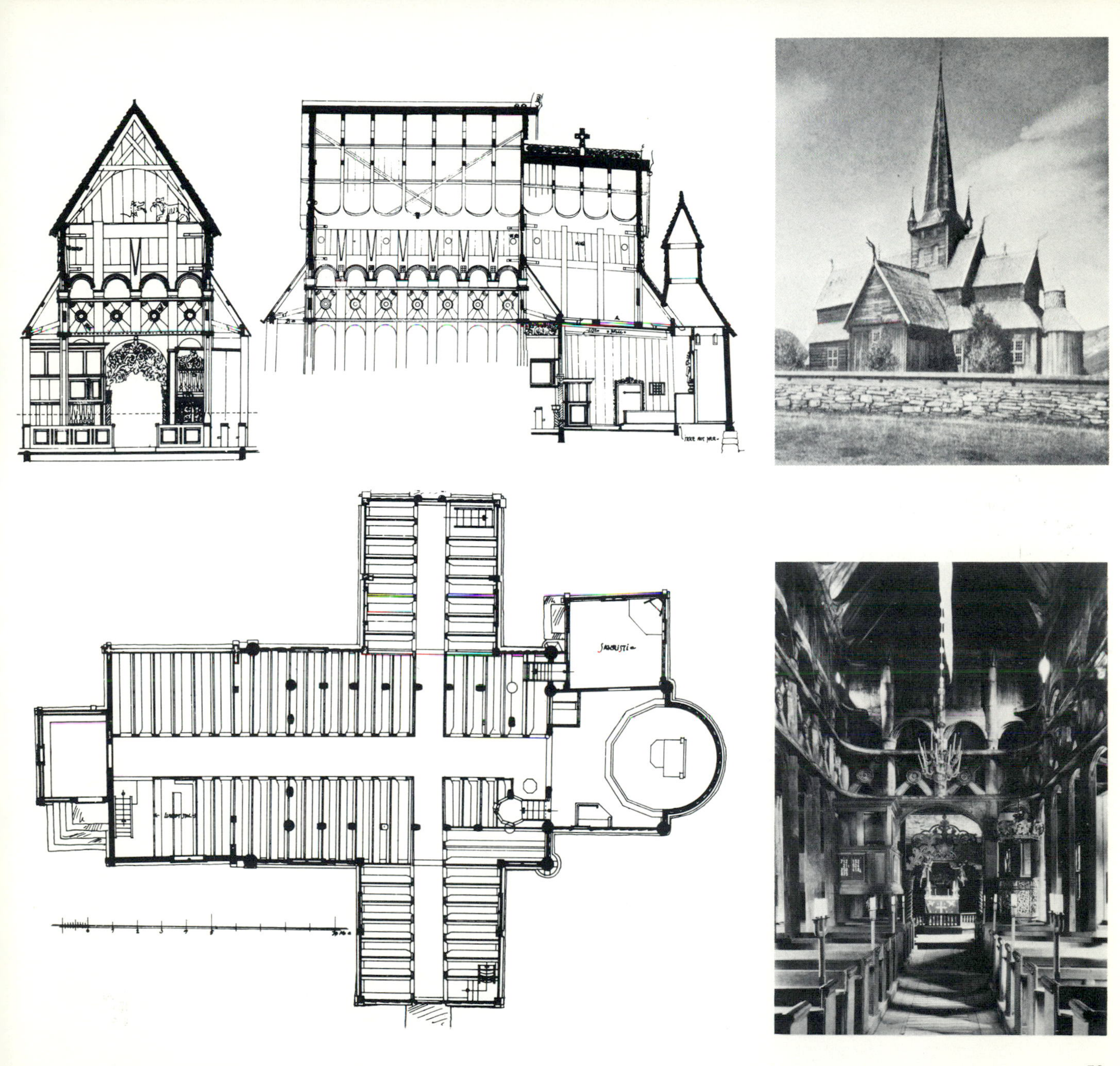

21. TORPO

As the church now stands, stripped of its chancel (1880) and pentices, it clearly reveals the idea of the «mast church»: the raised central section with gables beneath the saddle roof, the ambulatory with a sloping roof acting as a bracing round all four sides. The corner masts in the central section appear behind the shingles, the masts in between here, as usual, hewn flat on the outside and thus camouflaged behind the wall planks.

The demolished chancel had an apse, and a width equal to that of the nave. It dated back to the Middle Ages. When erected, however, the church had a narrower chancel, as indicated by the still present chancel arch. The subsequently built chancel had two masts running unobstructed to the floor, as in Kaupanger.

As in the latter, too, all free masts along the longitudinal walls of the nave also run down to the floor. As in Borgund, the short sides have four complete masts, as opposed to the five in the Kaupanger group (of which the central one is truncated, and rests on an arch).

Thus the construction in Torpo reveals features, some of which point to Kaupanger, others to Borgund. There are further traces of this in the details: the masts have block capitals, as in Urnes and Hopperstad, though not placed quite so high up, here beneath the lower arcade. Next follows the lower string beam, and cross-braces, as in Borgund, while the upper string beam is lacking. «Tongues» (splays on the masts) terminate at the lower string beam, whereas in the churches of the Borgund group they terminate at the upper one.

Apart from the position of the capitals, Torpo is consequently similar to Hopperstad, where string beams and cross braces, however, are later additions. In Torpo these are original. Accordingly it must be regarded as a link between the two groups.

Between the masts at the east end of the nave is stretched a barrel-vaulting canopy, representing the legend of the martyrdom of St Margaret, painted in the 13th century. Beneath this canopy, in catholic time, there was a lecturing gallery (se *Nore, Uvdal).*

Pews, resting on round-arched arcades, run along the outer walls. On the outside, the cornerposts of the ambulatory are seen to be covered with shingles, as far down as the point where the sloping roof above the demolished pentice abutted on it. The magnificent doorways, poorly protected, are exposed to the weather. – There has been a separate steeple, standing on the site of the new church. The belfry is of later date.

Plan, sectional drawings and sketch below showing the church as it appeared in 1880, with chancel and apse, but with no pentices. The original chancel was narrower.

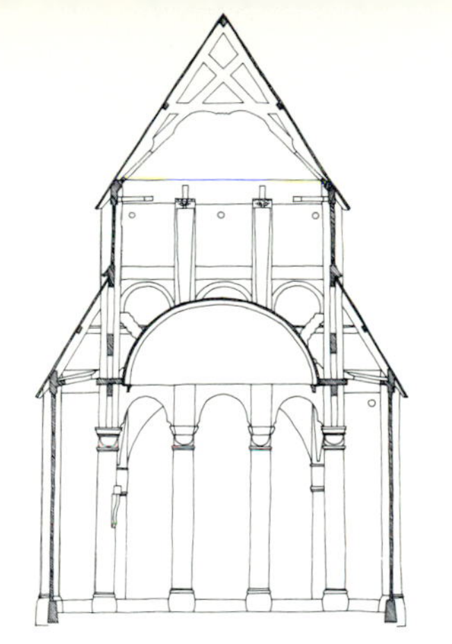
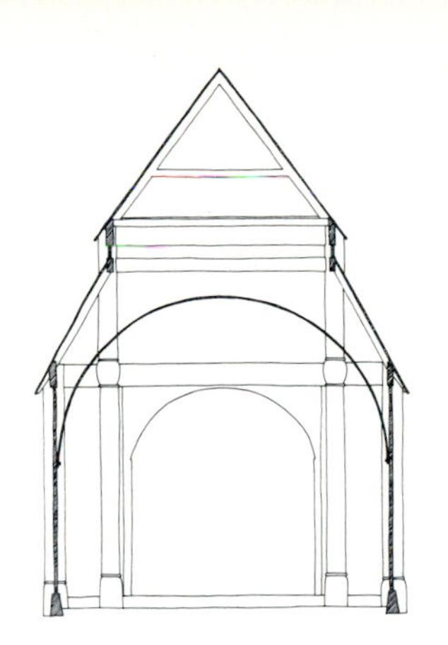

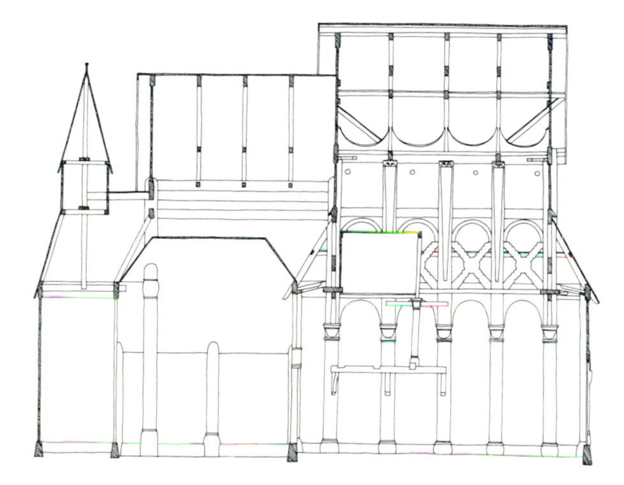
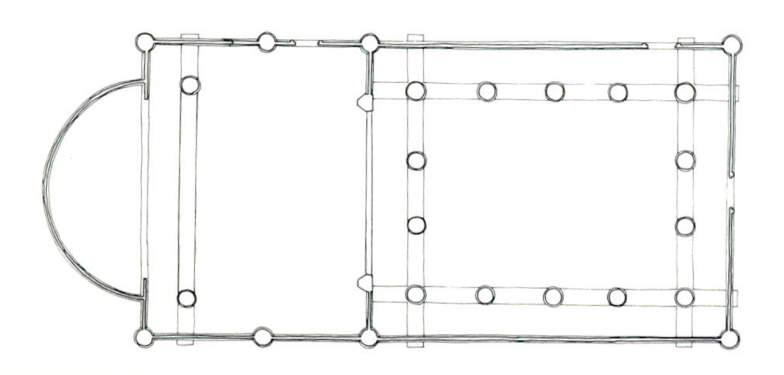

22. HEDDAL

Of the few mast churches in Telemark, this, the only one to have survived, towers majestically over the surrounding flat countryside: it is the largest of its kin, warranting its epithet «cathedral in wood».

In the nave of the church at Torpo, influence can be traced from the mast churches of both groups. In Heddal the chancel section points to Kaupanger, and the structure of the nave to Borgund. The explanation may be that the chancel, with its six free masts running down to the floor, has survived as a portion of the nave in an original church, while the twenty-masted nave and the chancel apse are subsequent additions, built approximately one hundred years later. From the outside we almost have the impression of two stave churches joined together.

The masts in the chancel have an elliptical cross-section, but a circular one near the floor. There are no string beams and cross-braces here (a single string beam now in position is new): everything is as in the Kaupanger nave, apart from the fact that in Heddal Church the masts are decorated at the top with masks.

In the nave the masts have a circular cross-section. On the longitudinal sides every second one runs down to the floor, so that we get, in fact, a further development of the Borgund system, which we also find in Ringebu. The Heddal nave has cross-braces and a lower string beam parallel, in this case, to Torpo. The capitals are undecorated cylinders, however, whereas the pediments to the lower, inserted arches are unusually pronounced. There is also double buttressing.

The church was given its present appearance as the result of radical restoration, or rather reconstruction, carried out by architects Blakstad and Munthe-Kaas in 1955, basing themselves on such mediaeval remains as had survived H.O. Nebelong's reconstruction a century earlier. Today, on antiquarian grounds, it is unlikely that Nebelong's work would have been interfered with, but there is no doubt that even his contemporaries objected to his «Wedding-cake Temple» (I.C. Dahl).

As far back as the 17th century the masts in the chancel had been cut, and a flat ceiling installed there and in the nave, in both cases supported by a central column. Nebelong removed this, and made his paraphrase.

The reconstruction of 1955 called the Middle Ages into existence: the chancel masts were extended right down to the floor, giving the chancel the appearance of a miniature stave-church nave with a raised central portion, buttressed masts, and an ambulatory. The wall decor is that of the 17th century. In the nave several masts, buttressing elements, and the roofing were resurrected to the best of the architects' ability or on the basis of preserved models. The carving in the doorway lacks the touch and exuberance to be found when the traditional pattern is adhered to.

Cross section and plan: After the restoration in 1955. Longitudinal section after conversion in 1850. Below The interior in 1837 (after I. C. Dahl/Schiertz).

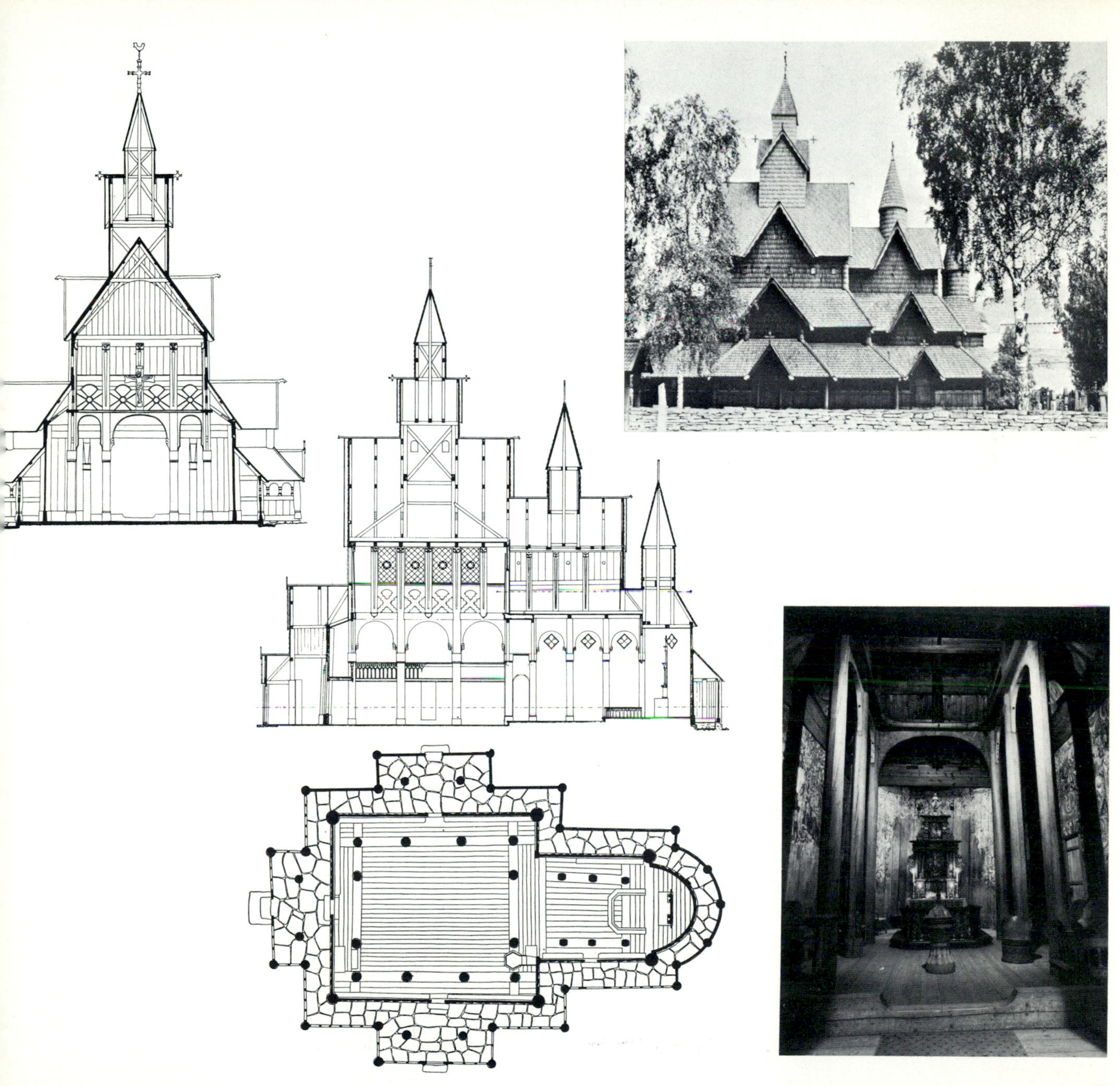

23. BORGUND

Of the fifteen surviving mast churches, Borgund is the only one which has been allowed to stand unchanged since the Middle Ages. This is probably the reason why it has served as a model for the restoration of several others. Pentices, ridge turret, the apse with its perivalium, as well as the entrance gables, are, however, here as in most early stave churches, said to be «Gothic» additions to a «Romanesque» core (nave with ambulatory, plus chancel, see ill. p. 18).

The main room of the church boasts fourteen masts, the central one of which on both longitudinal sides is truncated halfway down, resting on the lower of two sturdy flat rafters. This emphasizes the north–south direction at the expense of the traditional east–west axis, as does the fact that all masts in that alignment go down to the floor. At the same time the colonnade effect of the longitudinal sides is played down. The principle of doing away with middle masts can be traced further via the eight-mast (Gol/Hegge) to the four-mast (Hurum/Lomen) Valdres churches, where the bearer function of the *corner masts* is a principal motif. An interesting point is that all these churches can be shown to have the same plan and the samt number of masts, if the plan section is placed *above* the lower string beam.

The string beams with cross-braces strung between them, the splays («tongues») of the masts from the upper string beam up to the masks on top, the omission of details borrowed from stone architecture such as capitals and archivolt (see Urnes, Hopperstad, etc.), and extensive use of inserted brackets between the masts – all this contributes to emphasize the independence of the Borgund group as a supreme achievement in wood building.

The Borgund system offers far greater technical and formal freedom than the more classic approach of the Kaupanger group, and *may* be regarded as a further development of the latter. Also, it is conceivable that the builders of Borgund reverted to older models than the traditional, Christian ones abroad. If this is so, Borgund represents continuity, and Kaupanger/Urnes a stylistic interlude in Norwegian monumental wooden architecture.

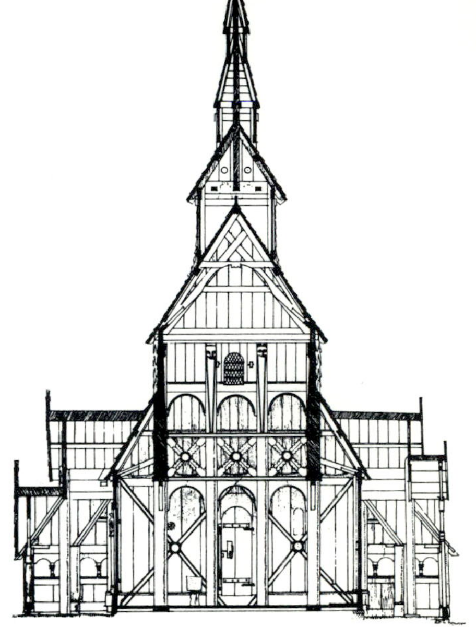

Few points of similarity with stone architecture, and not very like a basilica in construction: east–west axis broken by masts, and north–south axis emphasized by cutting the central mast.

The free-standing steeple is executed in the stave technique, with oblique masts familiar to us from annexed west towers in certain demolished stave churches (e.g. Årdal). The steeple may have been built at the same time as the church. Its open structure was later boarded over.

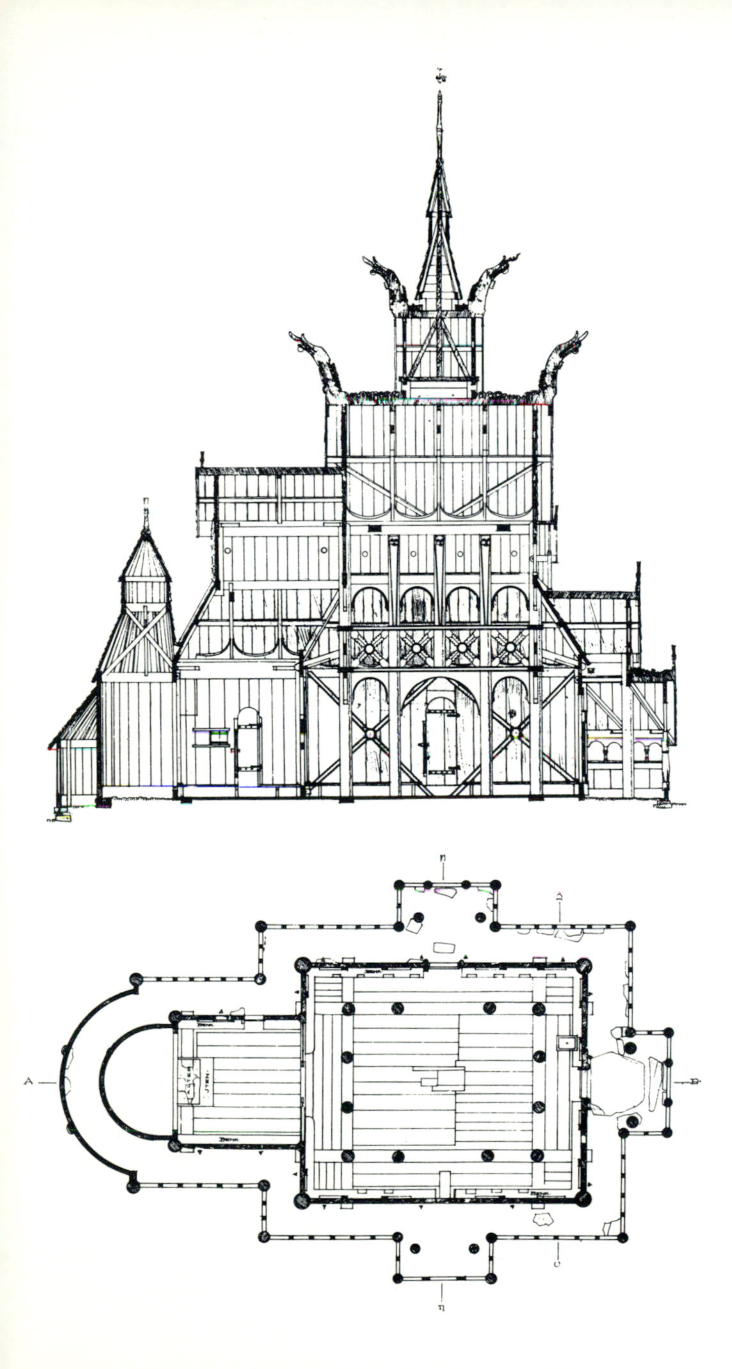

24. GOL

The use of string beams and cross-braces for stabilizing the masts gave the master builders of stave churches greater freedom than their predecessors, as well as offering fascinating opportunities for elaborating the triforium theme of ecclesiastical architecture, for developing double span, as in Ringebu and Heddal; for reducing the number of masts, as in Gol and Hegge, a feature exploited to the full in Hurum and Lomen.

The «forest of masts» from the Sogn churches is, as a conception, remote from the spacious interiors of the Valdres churches. Here the builder has struck out on his own, though following paths previously trodden either for non-ecclesiastical purposes, or influenced by different ecclesiastical inspiration, or impelled by the desire simply to experiment and create independently. The interior is less dominated axially, and more easily adaptable to use.

Hegge still serves the local parishioners; Gol has become a museum object. In 1884, in a somewhat derelict state, it was sold for demolition purposes, and moved to King Oscar II's collection at Bygdøy, from which the present-day Norwegian Folk Museum was developed.

The supporting skeleton in the nave, parts of the outer walls in the nave, and of the roofing, the chancel walls and the doors, of which the one at the south end had to be replaced by a replica, are all relics of the Middle Ages. Here, too, Borgund served as a model for reconstruction of the exterior (belfry, pentices, the exterior of the chancel, and entrance gables). Thus, in the chancel roof, we also recognise Borgund's «suspended» masts.

Of a total of fourteen masts in the nave, eight reach to the floor, grouped as in Hegge in pairs near the corners, on the longitudinal walls. The two middle masts to the east and the west are truncated and rest on the lower string beam, supported by semi-arched brackets.

The corner masts have cylindrical capitals decorated with carving, and all the masts are topped with masks, presumably the work of the craftsmen who decorated the church at Hegge. The lower quadrant brackets have pediments decorated with dragons.

The pentices can be seen to rest on the projecting ends of the ground frame of the nave, a solution as rare as it is logical, and one that was probably chosen during the process of restoration.

Chancel and apse contain wall paintings from the 1650s.

Plan drawing (after erection at Bygdøy) showing the ground frame running right out to the pentice wall. Opp. page, top: the church before it was moved.

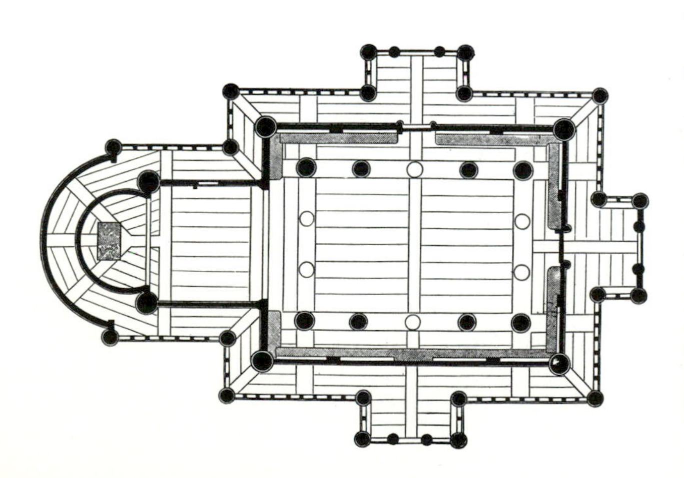

25. HEGGE

To get an idea of what this church may have looked like in mediaeval time, we might turn to Gol, where the various details (doorways, masks on masts, archipediments) point to the same master builder.

Today, these two churches have only the supporting skeleton of the main section in common: eight masts running down to the floor, while one mast on the longitudinal sides and two masts on the others rest on the lower string beam. Above this the truncated masts all continue to the bressummer supporting the roof, which in this way links together fourteen masts. This is the same number as in Borgund and Hurum/Lomen, with respectively twelve and four free masts reaching to the floor.

In the brightly painted interior of the church at Hegge the stave-church skeleton has the appearance almost of a decorative element, since its intention has been concealed and important details are missing.

When the church proved too small for its purpose, the services of Johs. Korpberget, a church builder from Gudbrandsdalen, were acquired. In 1807 he carried out the following changes:

On the lines of Lomen, in the neighbouring parish the plank wall in the body of the church was removed, and new outer walls in framework were erected flush with the former pentice walls, all under one roof. In the process the entire characteristic system of struts round the bearing masts, which are so essential to stability, and might be regarded as the mast churches' patent of nobility, disappeared.

The new «side aisles» acquired a sloping ceiling, and the main body of the church a flat one, level with the upper string beam. Above the ceiling the upper parts of the old nave can be studied at close quarters: the masts with their grotesque masks, the upper part of the former outer wall with its bull's-eyes, and the original trussed rafter roof. The upper arcade has double arches.

At the same time the nave was extended westwards, the prolonged roof being supported by four round masts with crude imitations of quadrant arches. The chancel, too, was widened to correspond with the original nave, whose eastern cornerposts, with traces of the nave's wall planking, had been preserved, and terminate the new chancel. Finally, a belfry with spire was erected.

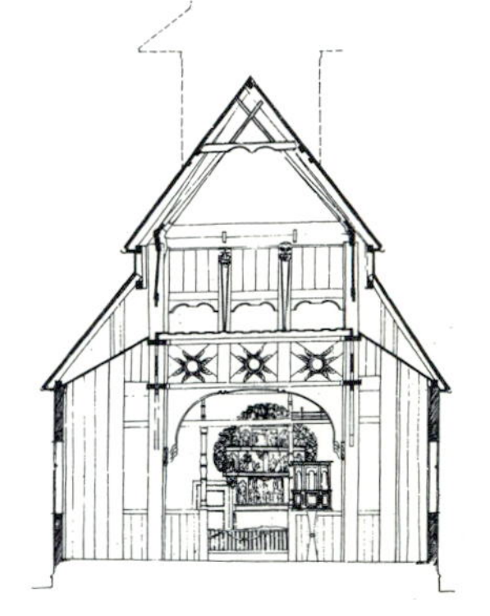

The mediaeval parts are more obvious in the sections than on the spot. The ceiling conceals the roof structure and vital parts of the sanctuary walls.

The old west door was moved with the entire west wall, while the outside doorway in the porch has been transferred from Fystrå Church.

The magnificent figural altar panel has been attributed to Øystein Kiørren, of Skjåk (1780). Belfry and porch are recent additions erected under the supervision of the architect Arnstein Arneberg.

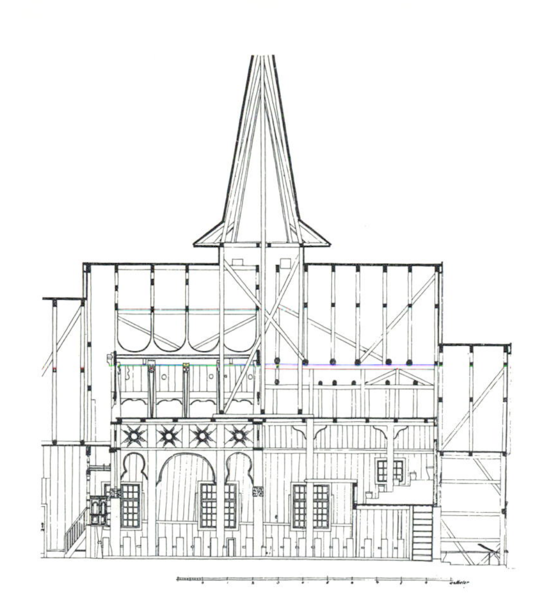

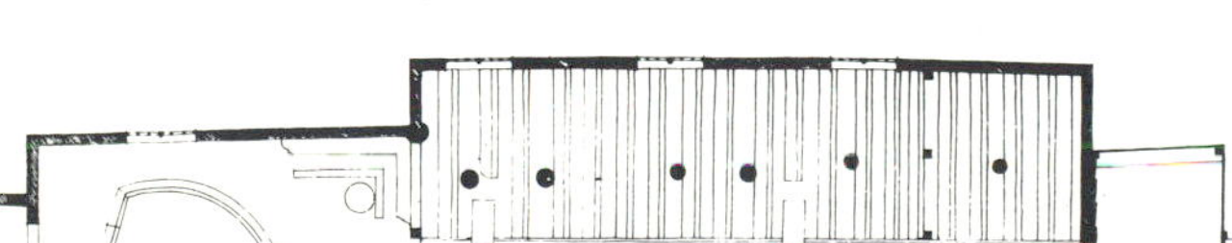

26. HURUM (Høre)

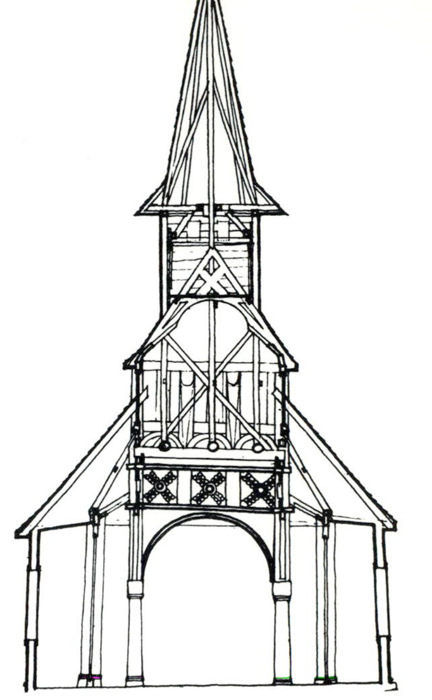

Sections showing the medieval building as a «church in the church», as in Lomen. At Hurum, however, the roof structure is concealed by the ceiling, and the entire medieval chancel has been removed.

This church has undergone changes similar to those at Hegge and Lomen, but in its exterior reveals more of the features of the stave church – the broken roof surface still betrays the mediaeval raised central space.

Hurum and Lomen are – or rather were – all of a piece. Their original elements show such striking similarities with Borgund that it is possible the same master builder was responsible.

Similarities included chancel and apse, and the construction of the central space from the top down to the lower string beam. The only deviation of significance here is seen to be the shape of the upper arches connecting the masts. While Borgund and Lomen here merely have a discreet moulding, Hurum has marked archivolts, which can be seen in the original, together with the preserved trussed rafter roof, above the recently installed ceiling in the nave.

As against Borgund's twelve free masts, Lomen and Hurum have only four reaching to the floor, one in each corner. Both in Lomen and in Hurum the cornerposts of the original nave wall are preserved, with connecting top bressummers and the system of buttressing the masts along all sides. A sloping ceiling, inserted in connection with the extension of 1822–23, is supported by the struts. In Hurum, as earlier in Hegge and Lomen, the mediaeval but hardly original pentice was removed on this occasion, and chancel and apse pulled down. Nothing remains of the Hurum chancel. The main room was widened by the width of the pentices, and extended towards the west. The stepped roof profile was to some extent preserved in the nave. In the new, wider chancel the same effect was produced by means of an artifice, structurally unfounded.

From the Middle Ages the chancel arch, with its mask-decorated posts, has been preserved, as well as the carved pillars of the rood screen, with their more recent decorated painting. The upper member is of later date. The original west door has been incorporated in the new west wall, while the south doorway has been placed in the porch. The four supporting masts have tendril-decorated cylindrical capitals, as in Lomen, Hegge, and to some extent Gol. Otherwise the interior is in untreated wood, with the mediaeval mouldings lined in black.

Hurum Church has a free-standing belfry (1732) of a type similar to that in Lomen, and also to the one of the stone church at Slidre. Parts of the original ridge turret – similar to the one on the roof at Borgund – have been incorporated in the lychgate.

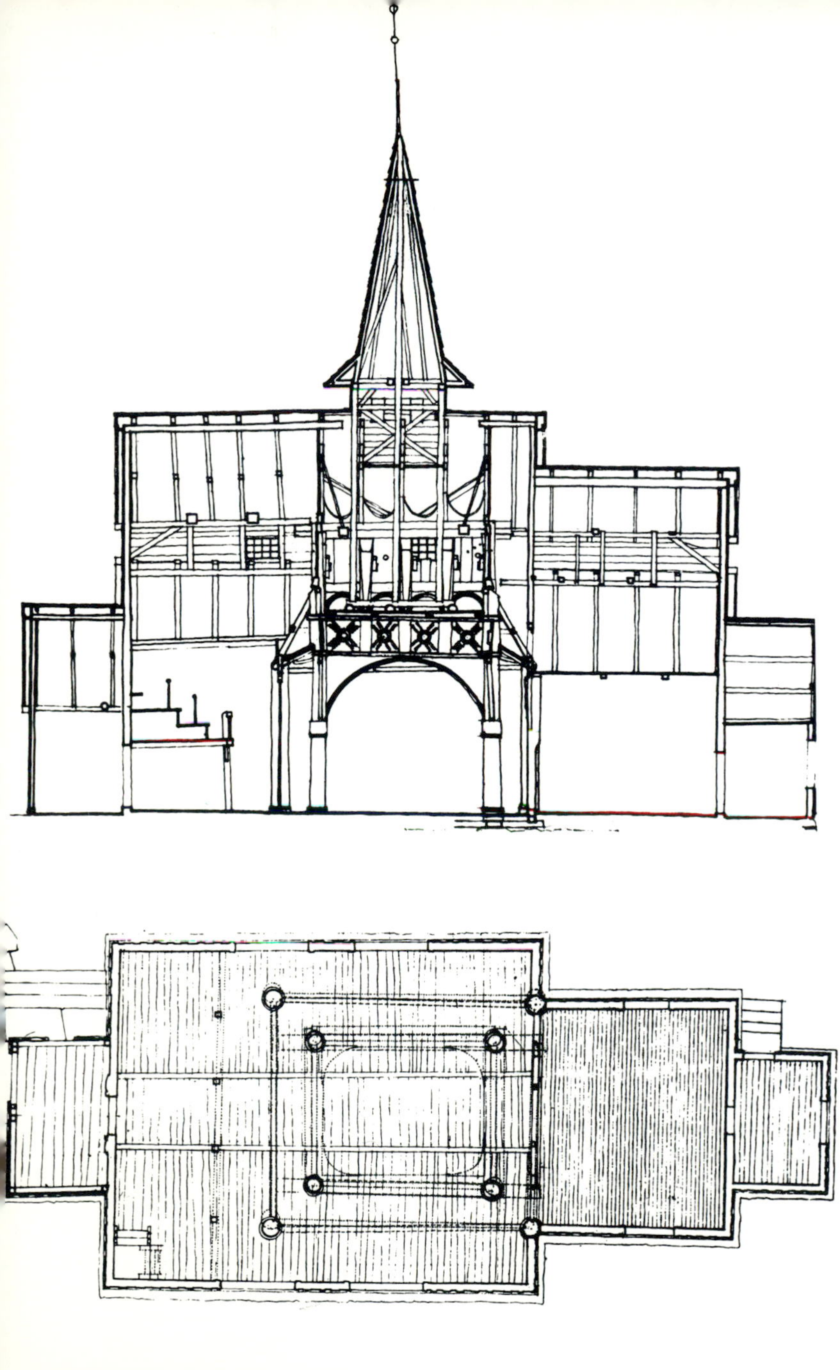

27. LOMEN

Like its neighbours at Hurum and Hegge, Lomen has had to renounce a great deal of the Middle Ages in order to survive, but has nevertheless not forfeited its noblest parts – the supporting skeleton.

In the extended, light interior, with galleries along two sides, this can be studied in detail.

Of the total of fourteen masts above the lower string beam («triforium» height), only the four corner masts reach to the floor. To support the others, and to buttress the entire system, we find sturdy wooden arches inserted between the corner masts, beneath the lower string beam.

The upper part of the nave, with its mediaeval trussed rafter roof, seems to be hovering in the semi-darkness above – the stave church in its traditional form challenged by new impulses. As at Hegge and Hurum, the corner masts have cylindrical capitals, only slightly thicker than the masts themselves – from the point of view of building in wood more logical than the block capitals to be found in several stave churches.

The cornerposts of the nave have also been preserved, with slots for the plank walls that bounded the original sanctuary. A corresponding slit can be seen in the bressummer, which is connected with the fourteen masts by means of the ingenious belt of buttressing arches all the way round.

Outside there is little to suggest the stave church. About 1750 – maybe not until after 1800 – the sanctuary was widened by the breadth of the pentices, as well as being extended to the west. The west door followed suit, while the one-time south doorway was inserted into a new porch. Above all this an unbroken slated roof was stretched and the new walls were panelled – to the annoyance of the then incumbent, Ruge, who was an antiquarian born before his time. By now the conversion, too, has acquired the patina of age, and has added value to the venerable building.

On that occasion the chancel, too, was extended, and given the same width as the previous sanctuary. Strangely enough, the roofing of the old chancel, which reveals certain points of similarity with that of Borgund, including the «hovering» chancel masts, is still in position. The south doorway in the mediaeval chancel was placed in a small porch in the new one.

The church at one time had an apse, in common with the pentice an addition made shortly after building. The belfry was erected in 1674. As in several other churches in the valley, the lower, wider part is log built, with a sloping roof, the upper, narrower portion built partly in log, partly in stave technique, with a slated saddle roof and openwork wooden gables. The result is a variation in miniature on the theme of the stave church.

The whole skeleton of the mediaeval church, with the roof structure, stands intact in the extended sanctuary. This gives an intense feeling of the strength of stave church structure. The mediaeval roof structure can be seen preserved above the more recent chancel.

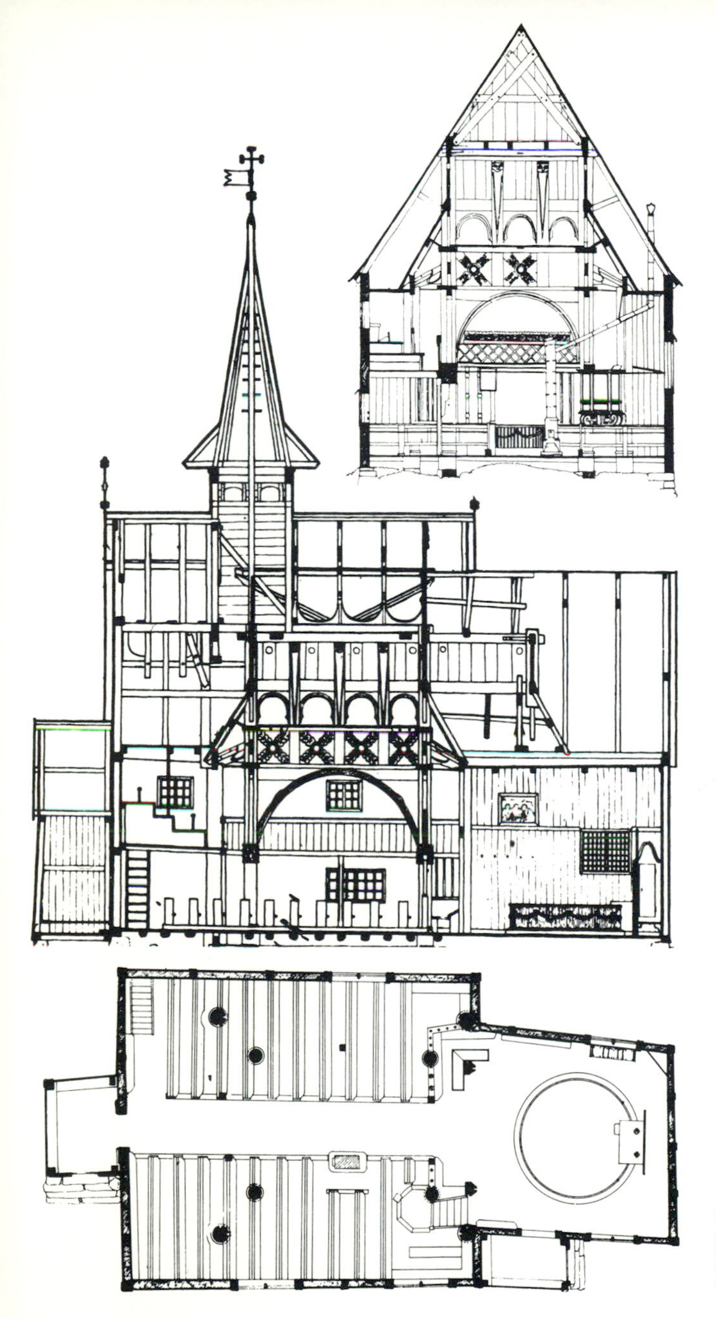

28. FLESBERG

A painting from 1701, simple but meticulous in execution, reveals a fully developed stave church of the mast type, with a pentice and an apse furnished with a turret. Roof, walls, and visible posts are covered with shingles. Small windows are to be seen in the outer walls of the main central space, and also cornermasts in nave and chancel beneath the upper roof. The other free masts in the nave, assuming there were at one time intermediate masts, are here as elsewhere flattened on the outside, and concealed beneath the external boarding.

Today practically all we can recognise from the picture is the enclosure formed of upended flagstones. However, after a conversion in 1735 the nave of the original stave church was preserved, constituting the west wing of a cruciform church. In the nave, only the surrounding plank walls with cornerposts and sills have been preserved – the free masts were removed, together with the roof structure which gave way to a flat ceiling. Finally, the west door – which shows similarity with Nore and Attrå (demolished) – has survived, painted and hacked about.

A date of 1683 has been assigned to the pulpit and 1745 to the altar panel. A complete restoration of the original colours was undertaken recently. The tower dates back to 1792.

From the outside can be seen the projecting ends of the ground frame in the nave. Photographs taken in 1956, when a new floor was laid, show mortices for masts at the intersections.

The short sides of the ground frame have no holes, and the longitudinal sides have been cut away, making it impossible to decide whether there were any intermediate masts. Signs, however, tend to indicate a four- or eight-mast church.

The plan drawing on this page shows a plausible position for the masts. Main plan drawing showing the truncated ground frame which is still to be found beneath the church, and is visible from the outside. Apart from the portal and the outer wall in the nave, this is the only mediaeval feature to have survived.

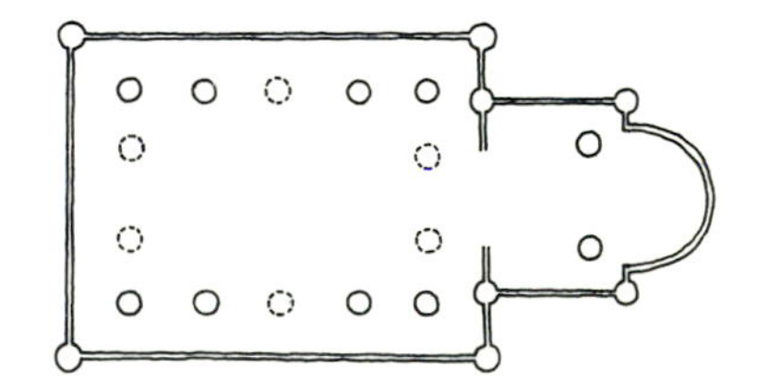

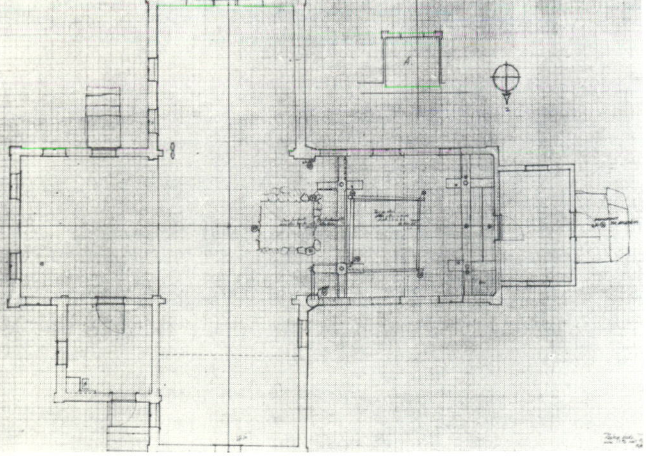

29. RINGEBU

From its elevated position in the hills this church looks out across the surrounding countryside, facing the mediaeval «Guild's plain».

As at Lom, here, too, the tower, which is high-spired and has finials, and the transepts are the work of Werner Olsen (1631). He again employs timbers upright, but unlike Lom the wings of Ringebu do not break the outer wall in the mediaeval *nave,* but in the *extension* of the nave to the east, beneath the tower. We are dealing with real *transepts,* which have also the same height as the nave, and like it a stepped roof profile, with the same roof angles. He also added a chancel, giving it the same height, very nearly the same width, and profile.

Seen from the outside the chancel gives the church the air of a true «basilica», but the worthy masterbuilder Werner was incapable of carrying out this idea in the interior. For buttressing the tower and the raised central part of the chancel, which have no throughgoing masts, he inserted a layer of beams level with the lower string beam, over the entire church.

In the nave this was removed when restoration took place in 1922. This again revealed the mediaeval trussed rafter roof and nave. Its construction shows similarities with Heddal: the four masts of the longitudinal sides running down to the floor support double spans, with intermediate masts cut off at the lower string beam. Ringebu, however, has string beams both above and beneath the cross-braces, and the masts carry cylindrical capitals, in fact at two levels. Heddal has five masts on the short sides, of which the middle one has been truncated, clearly to link up the nave with the long and impressive chancel. Like Borgund, Ringebu, however, has four masts at the east and west ends, all running down to the floor. Against the chancel the two middle ones were at one time cut off. The horseshoe shape of the arcades have an almost Moorish effect.

The longitudinal walls of the nave have two intermediate posts, which show traces of wings in the central field. These were either original or else were added shortly after building, and may have served as side chapels. They must have been removed at an early stage, and their plank walls used for filling in the walls of the longitudinal nave. Apart from the small one mast church at Nore, wings from the Middle Ages are known to us in the demolished stave church at Ål.

It has been shown that Ringebu Church had pentices. The west door shows traces of Sogn, but must be of more recent date.

The altar panel was carved in 1686 by Johs. Skraastad, one of the early masters of «gristle» Baroque, and the pulpit in 1703 by Lars Borg. The drapery painting of the inside walls is from about 1720.

The free-standing, log-built steeple is post-Reformation.

The longitudinal section shows the mediaeval nave (right) and (left) W. Olsen's method of extending the basilical idea to the chancel, with a central tower. – Top n.p.: wings in the demolished church at Ål, from the Middle Ages.

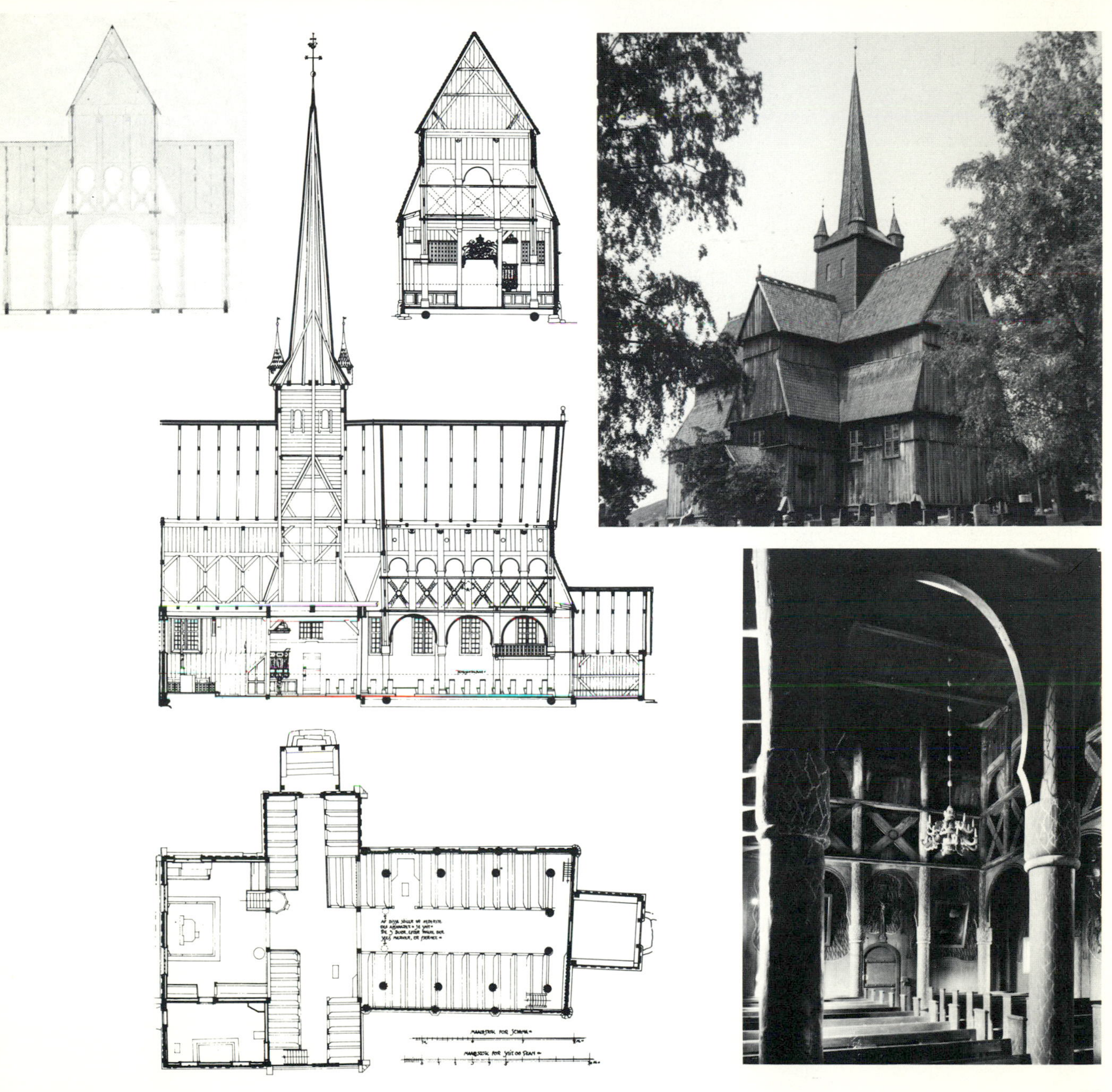

30. VÅGÅ

The stave churches are all from the the Middle Ages. In later wooden churches use was made preferably of the rather prosaic notched log technique, generally becoming more familiar to craftsmen.

Vågå Church was new built in 1627, as a wooden skeleton with upright planking, in fact in the spirit of the stave church. The difference is to be found rather in the technical and formal details than in principle.

Thus, the entire west wall in the former stave church (presumably a single-nave building), was without difficulty incorporated in the new west front.

The planks of the west wall, together with a number of others, some of which have archaic embellishments, have given the building both the label and the superficial features of a stave church. The masterbuilder was Werner Olsen (*obit.* 1682), the son of a clergyman from Ringsaker, who also supervised the extensions to the stave churches at Lom and Ringebu, in the same technique.

In the plan the church at Vågå is cruciform, with a central tower, spire and finials, supported by free-standing square-hewn posts.

On the outside one perceives a clear marking of the skeleton and the fine proportions, inside the extensive use of open braces, which are alien to Norwegian mediaeval stave-building technique.

This suggests a southerly influence, that of English and continental framework-building, as does the gable field, which is slightly corbelled but panelled.

The vestry is an independent, log-built addition.

The mediaeval blind arcades of the west wall are obvious imitations of stone, while the pilasters by the west entrance and the doorway in the southern transept, with its dominant animal ornamentation, are reminiscent of the Urnes style.

Section showing diagonal struts in the outer wall, a feature otherwise unknown in stave church architecture. Below: the west wall of the stave church, inserted in west front of 1627.

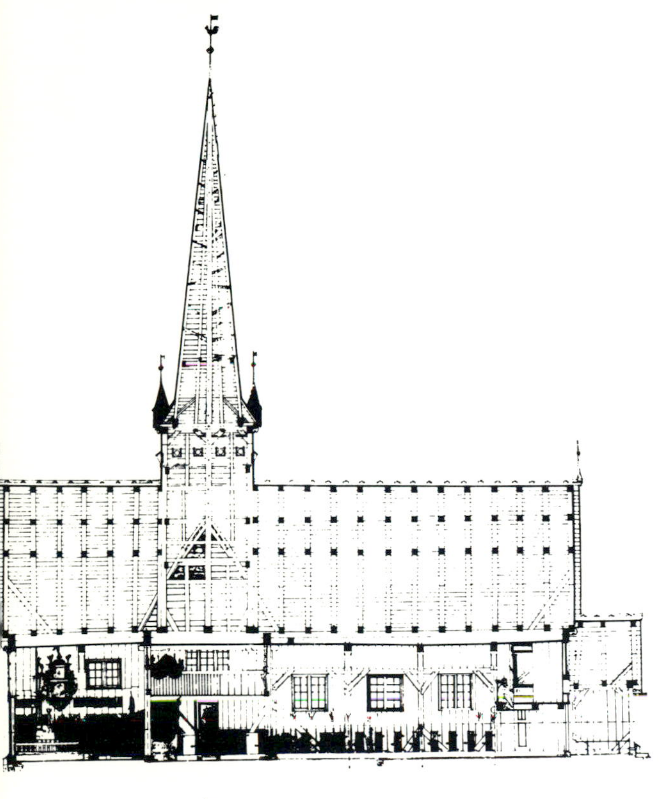

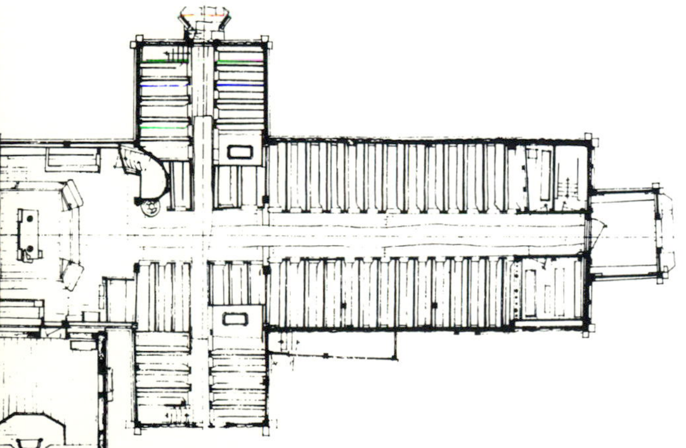

1 2 3 4

5

1. Borgund.

2. Torpo. Canopy from the 13th century.

3. Ål. Mask from mast in the nave.

4. Borgund.

6. Hopperstad: View through chancel door towards the nave.

7.–8. Hopperstad. Canopy over side altar. 14th century.

9.–10. Kaupanger. Chancel ceiling.

11. Kaupanger. Bracing of masts against outer wall in the nave.

12. Eidsborg. Entrance door in the pentice.

13. Kaupanger. Link between chancel and nave.

14. Reinli. «Suspended» mast.

6
7
8
9
10
11
12
13
14

COMPARATIVE PLANS

The plans are all in the same scale and show mediaeval parts.

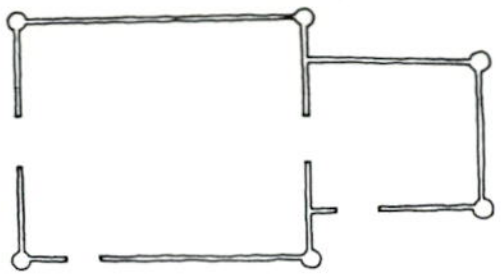

1. Holtålen

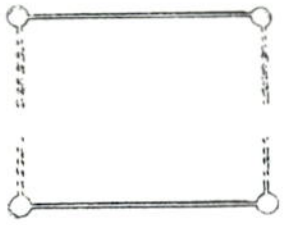

2. Underdal

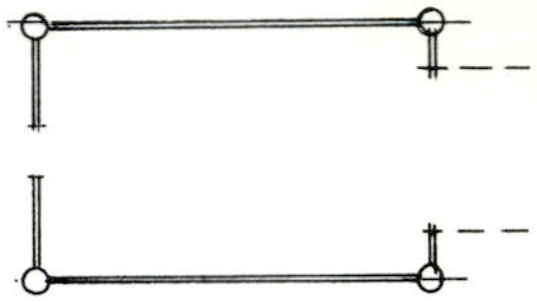

3. Rollag

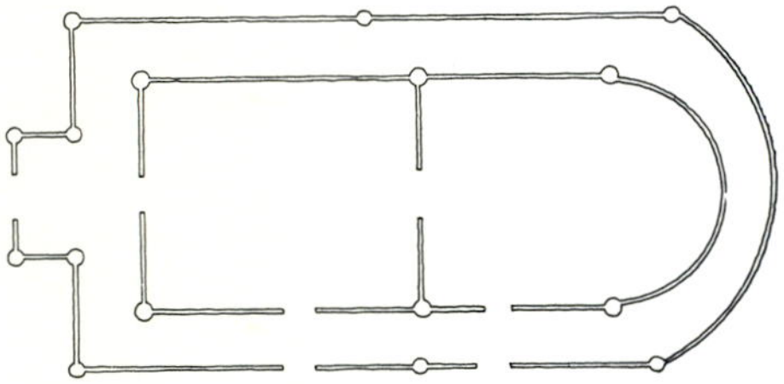

4. Reinli

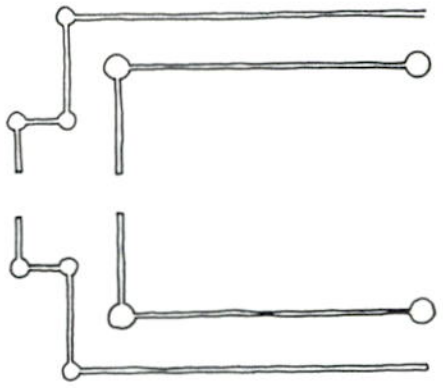

5. Hedal

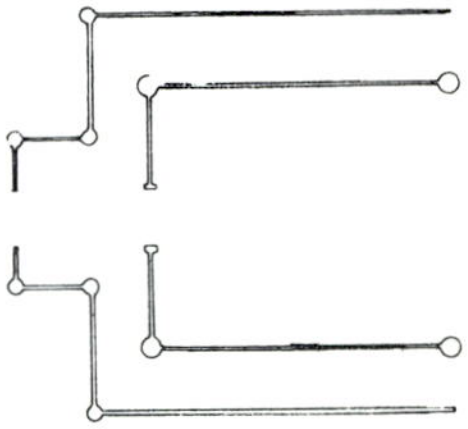

6. Eidsborg

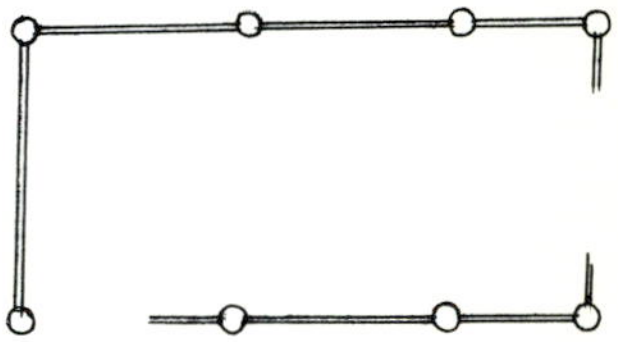

7. Grip

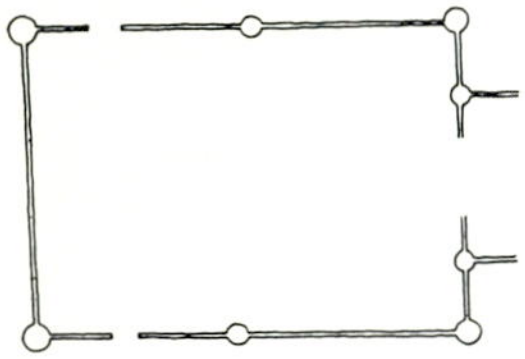

8. Rødven

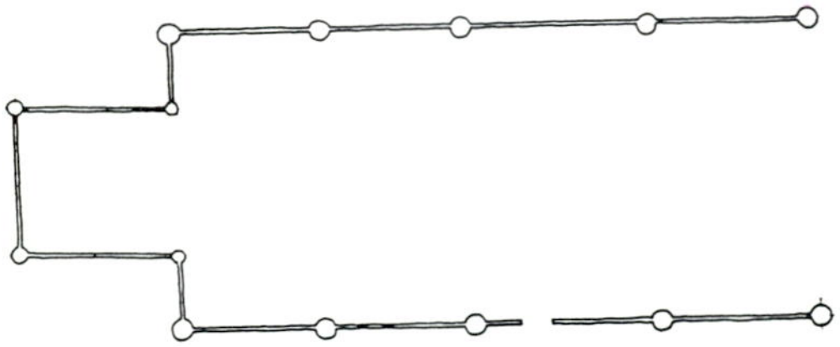

9. Kvernes

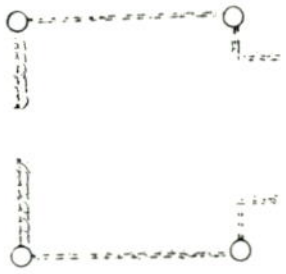

10. Garmo

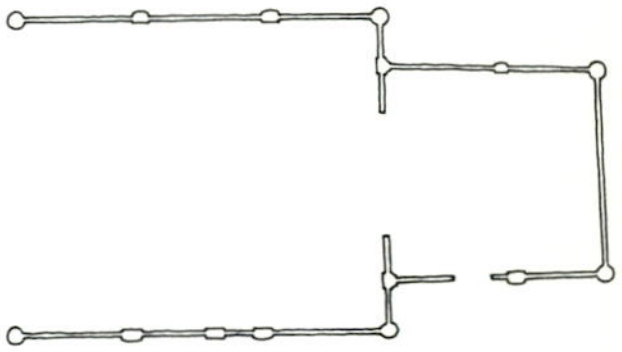

11. Røldal

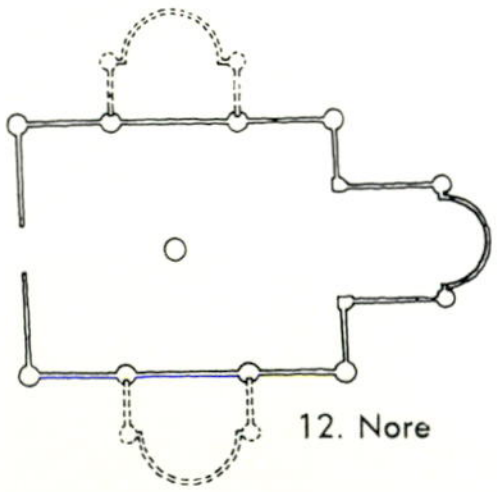

12. Nore

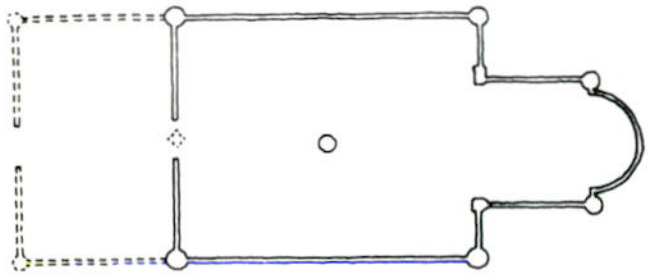

13. Uvdal

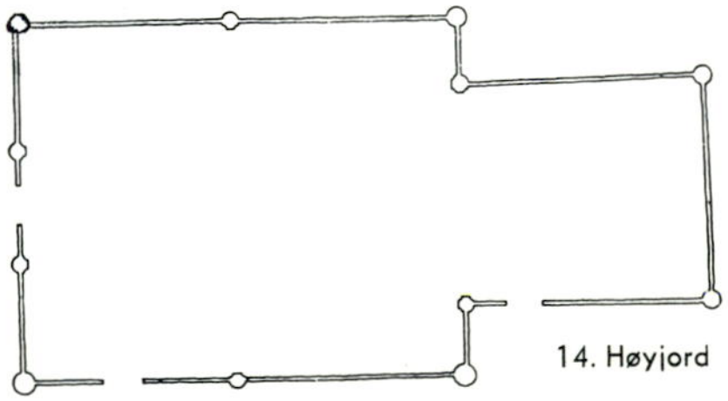

14. Høyjord

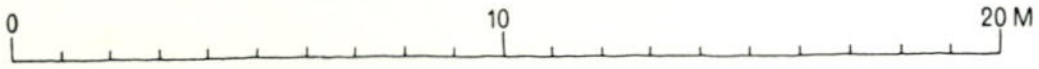

0 10 20 M

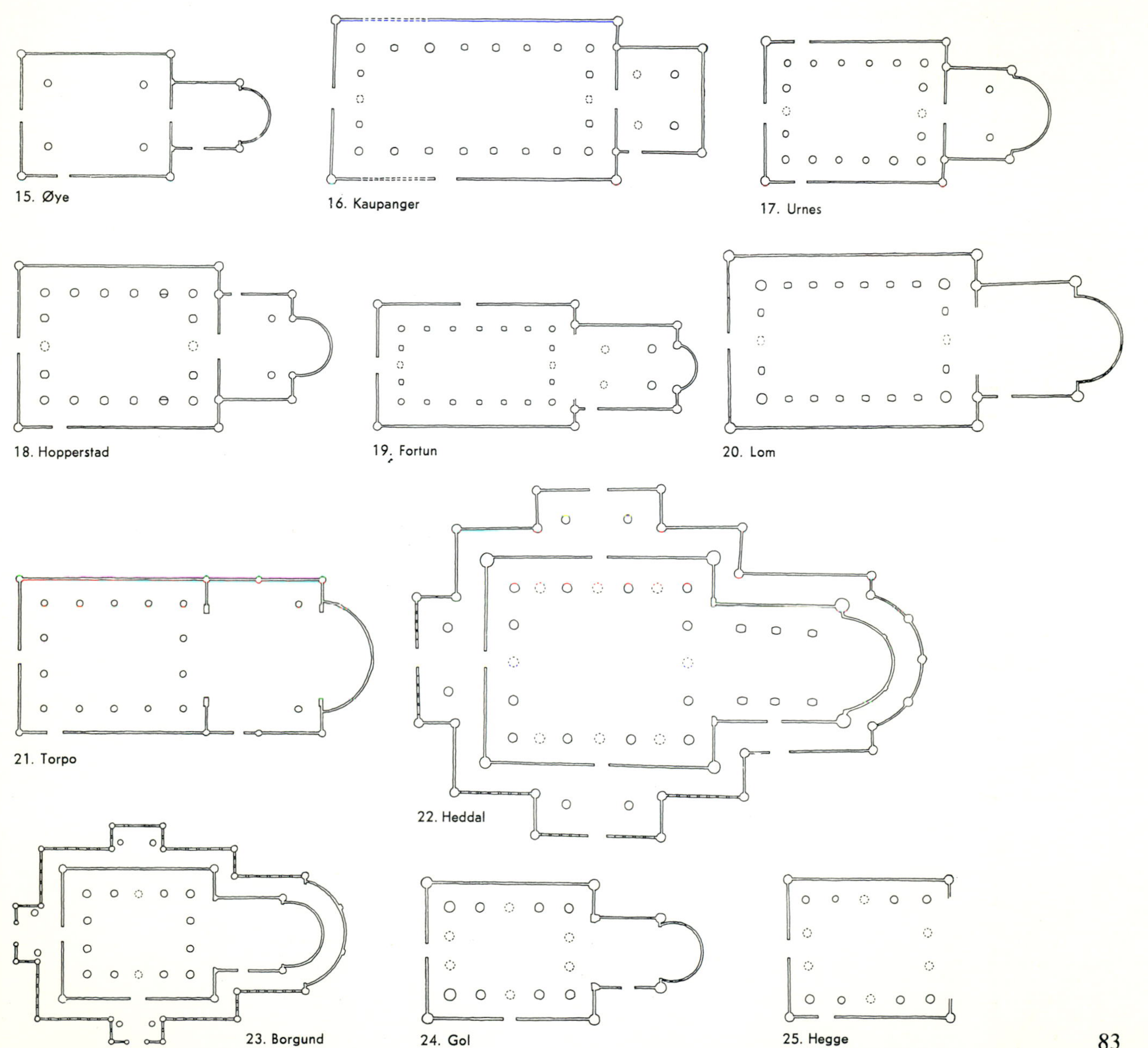
15. Øye
16. Kaupanger
17. Urnes
18. Hopperstad
19. Fortun
20. Lom
21. Torpo
22. Heddal
23. Borgund
24. Gol
25. Hegge

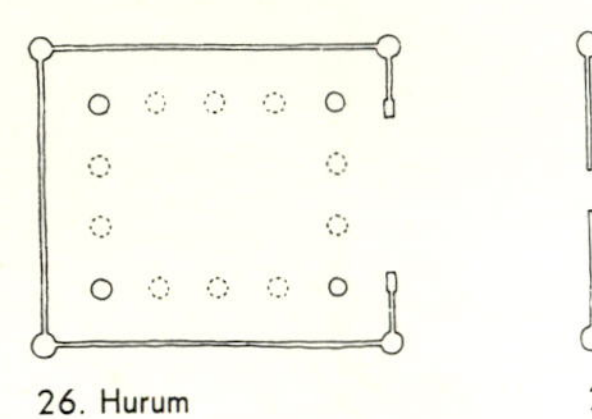
26. Hurum

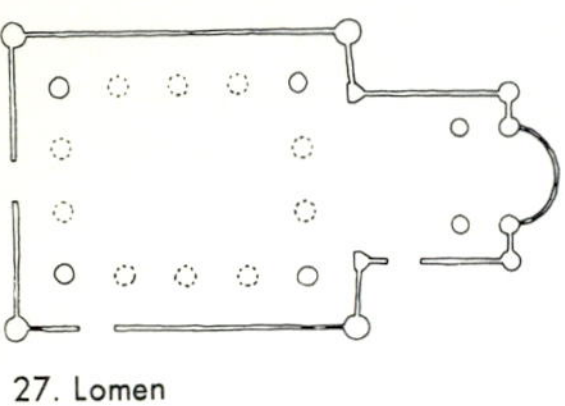
27. Lomen

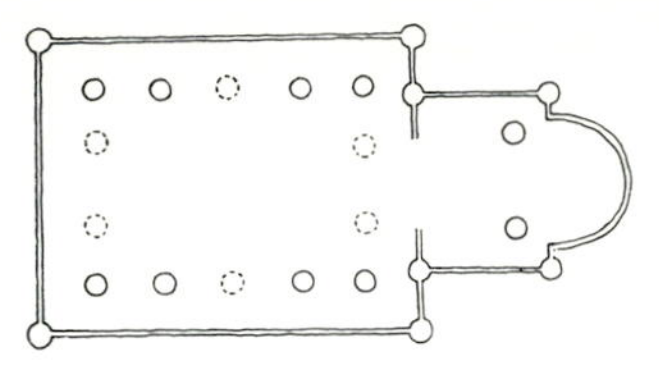

28. Flesberg

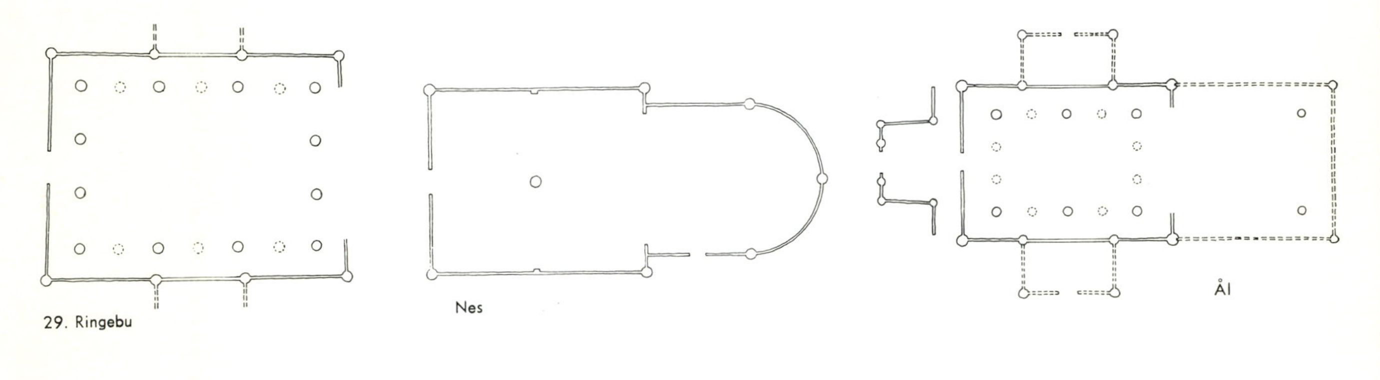
29. Ringebu

Nes

Ål

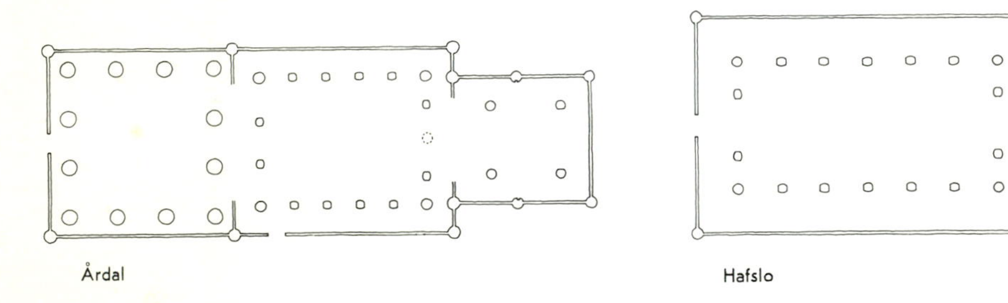
Årdal

Hafslo

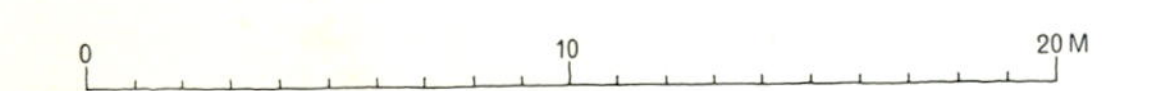